Your Phone Connection

Versus

IØØ78444

Your Prayer Connection

You have a phone line; do you have a prayer line?

By
Joseph Blessing Omosigho
Author of the best seller *Knocked Down But Not Knocked Out*

Foreword by Pastor Enoch A. Adeboye
General Overseer of The Redeemed Christian Church of God

Your Phone Connection Versus Your Prayer
Connection
Copyright © 2006, 2009 by Joseph B. Omosigho
Written by Joseph Blessing Omosigho
Cover design by Emmanuel Ogiozee
Foreword by Pastor Enoch A. Adeboye

Printed in the United States of America
Published by The Ministry of Christ
ISBN 978-0-9794876-0-6
ISBN 978-1-935529-03-3

FOREWORD

Prayer is our mandatory duty as children of God. If we are to experience revival in these last days, we must pray. The apostle Paul told us to "pray without ceasing" (1 Thess. 5:17).

It is fascinating that these days; people are becoming more attached and connected to their phones than they are to God through prayer and Bible study. Prayer is our spiritual phone connection to God.

Pastor Joseph Blessing Omosigho has fulfilled his God-given assignment by writing this book. Read this book prayerfully. It will help you develop a personal connection and a passionate relationship with God in your prayer life. It is important that you and I give to God our best when it comes to love, commitment, and prayer.

I encourage you to be firmly and faithfully connected to God. I thank God for this book; it will certainly bless you, transform you, and positively change your prayer life experience. May your physical phone connection not become a distraction to your spiritual (prayer) connection to God, in Jesus' name. Amen!

Pastor Enoch A. Adeboye
General Overseer
The Redeemed Christian Church of God

DEDICATION

This miracle revival prayer book is dedicated to our Lord God Almighty, our Manufacturer, King, and Jehovah, whose written Word is our life manual and constitution.

ACKNOWLEDGEMENTS

I give all the glory to the Lord Emmanuel and thank my family—my wife, Gloria; David; Samuel; and Hannah—for their love and support. I also thank everyone who assisted and supported this work, one way or another. May the good Lord bless and support you all in your individual areas of need, in Jesus' name.

Special thanks to Pastor Chryss Okonofua and his church family for inviting me to preach in their church. God gave me the revelation of this book while I was in prayer, asking Him what He wants me to tell His people. This revelation has literarily changed and transformed the prayer life experience of so many people since the day it was first preached and taught at, the Tower of Love Parish of The Redeemed Christian Church of God in Texas, United States of America.

My humble prayer is that this book will remain a prayer life-changer by the grace of God to the glory of God alone.

TABLE OF CONTENTS

INTRODUCTION

God is about to set your prayer life on fire and set you apart for His mighty works in these last days. After reading this book, your prayer life will never be the same again. Never again will Satan be able to hinder your prayers or God's replies. Instead, you will be empowered to invade the enemy's camp and take back all that he has stolen from you. Starting today, anytime you embark on a prayer mission, the heavens will stand at attention because they will know that the Master's child is on the line, waiting to hear from the Father of all Spirits, the King of Kings and Lord of all.

Anytime you take prayer for granted, you also are taking your life and family for granted. If you long for more of God and less of you, you must tarry in the place of prayer until you are endued with power from on high. Just as your phone connection helps you connect with other people, your prayer connection will help you develop an intimate relationship with God.

God has always used the power of prayer to transform the lives of His people. Those who tarry in His presence He has anointed with an unusual grace, and they have to transform the world by bringing His glory down to earth and quenching the fiery darts of the evil one. Do you want to be one of these people? Are you ready? Then prepare to enter our Maker's presence. . . .

Chapter 1

What Is a Phone?

Prayer is a life experience. Human knowledge does not determine the power of prayer; the knowledge of God does. God will honor any prayer prayed from a sincere heart, prayed by faith, and prayed in obedience to His Word. You do not have to know the entire Bible before you can pray; your mustard seed faith will be sufficient. If the power of prayer were based on human knowledge (education), someone like me, would not have access to God.

I thank God that faith, love, peace, and hope cannot be bought for a price. They are developed, conceived and born out of a meaningful relationship with God and truly knowing that God is our Father. I have seen both uneducated and educated men accomplish great things for God through prayer. I also have seen well educated and uneducated people try to figure God out by reasoning and not by faith. When it comes to prayer, God honors our faith, the cleanliness of our hearts, and obedience—not our race, color, nationality, background, or earthly or educational status.

To help you understand the importance of prayer as communication with God, let's first look at the telephone. Prayer and the telephone serve similar purposes; the difference is with whom you are communicating.

What Is a Phone?

The word *phone* is a short form of the word *telephone*. It is a device used for communication between two or more people. It came into existence through technological advancement and invention. Let us take a brief look at the words *tele* and *phone* to be able to articulate the full meaning of the word *telephone*.

"**Tele**" means to talk, to tell, and to communicate. Telegraph and telegram were the first communication devices introduced as a means of communication before the telephone was invented.

"**Phone**" is a process; it is the conversion of words into waves through the combination of sound and tune, propelled by an electronic device, and connected to a server or a network that converts the sounds back into words. After the conversion, you will hear the speaker on the other side as if the person speaking is physically standing before you.

A Brief History of the Telephone

Alexander Graham Bell invented the telephone in 1870 with the help of his assistant, Watson Thomas. He invented a device that could transmit voice (words) into sound, and sound into an electronic wave. The electronic wave is transmitted through the service of a network server that converts sound to tunes and then back into words. In the past, telephone gadgets were big machines with big switchboards operated by manpower. The invention of the telephone was a huge breakthrough for human communication. The first communication connection device was a one-way deal. After a period of time, the telephone eventually evolved into a two-way communication device as technology grew and advanced, giving birth to a new technological era in the world of communication.

Wireless Phones

After many years of research, wireless communication devices came into existence, which led to the introduction of cell phones. The migration of the communication industry into the wireless communication era began in 1947. The first public presentation of wireless phones was in 1979 in Tokyo, Japan. The telecommunications industry has come a long way; you and I are enjoying the labor and sacrifices of its inventors. Those inventors were full of passion, willing to go the extra mile to research and bring comfort and fun to the telecommunications world. Today millions of cell phones are sold yearly and thousands are manufactured monthly for the world to enjoy, including the latest of them all—the Internet phone (aka, the iPhone). Telecommunications has come to stay and will remain with us as long as we live, until the second coming of Jesus Christ.

Chapter 2

What Is Prayer?

Prayer is our spiritual line of communication to God by faith through the power of His Spirit in the light of His Word. Prayer is one of the greatest parts of our praise and worship to God, when we come before Him with an attitude of thanksgiving, appreciation, and adoration to glorify the name of the one and only true God. Prayer is entering into the throne of grace in the light of His love as we bow before His awesome presence in humility, declaring His lordship over our lives, the works of our hands, and the powers that there are and will be forever.

Just as the telephone is a means of communication between humans, so is prayer with the divine Being. Prayer is a combination of thoughts and words expressed by faith. Prayer is both verbal and non-verbal. Prayer was first introduced in the form of sacrifices of praise, thanksgiving, and worship on an altar, on which an animal or the fruits of the ground were presented to God. In Genesis chapter 4, Cain brought his fruits of the ground and Abel brought a lamb to offer sacrifices to God. Prayer has since developed into the human element of existence, which imparts the total man—spirit, soul, and body; thus, we offer our **"bodies as living sacrifices"** as we pray

(Romans 12:1 NIV). Prayer breakthroughs began as a result of the death of Jesus Christ on the cross, when He became our ultimate sacrifice. His death and resurrection strengthened our relationship with God, as we find favor with Him. Today we are adopted children of God, accepted in the beloved.

Let us break down the word *prayer*, just as we did *telephone*, as we employ the Spirit of God to guide us into the word of life and open the eyes of our understanding, in Jesus' name. The word *prayer* could be divided into two parts: **"PRA"** and **"YER."**

"Pra" means to talk to or to request of. It also could mean to prepare to worship or to come before. A breakdown of the letters will give us a fuller meaning.

P: To **p**resent oneself before the throne of grace.
R: To **r**everence, to **r**elate to, to **r**equest of, and to **r**ender.
A: To **a**dore, to **a**lign with, to **a**dmit to, and to **a**llow or to give **a**ll. It is like saying to God, "Not my will, but Your will be done, O Lord."

"Yer" means to respond to the **"pra"** that was offered from the human world or prayer request. **"Yer"** is a confirmation of what you are grateful for, seeking, and your prayer request. Let us break down the letters.

Y: **Y**our word, as God's spoken word or written Word. The best form of prayer is to pray in line with God's word, thus quoting His word back to Him. His word becomes the anchor of your prayer because God cannot deny Himself.
E: When you speak, your words are translated into an **e**cho, just as the phone is propelled by electronic waves, but this echo is a spiritual wave. When you pray, you must pray with

expectation, which forms the basis of your faith, the evidence or your hope. Therefore, as you pray (echo), your requisitions, or prayers, will go before the Effendi (Greek word for "Master").

R: After you pray, God will respond to your prayers **(pra)** by receiving them. God receives all our prayers **(pra)**, but runs them through the processing filter of His plan and will for our lives. God's response to each of our prayers is based upon His plan and purpose for our lives, except in the case of His permissive will, when we are responsible for the consequences.

Your prayer line, or your prayer connection, will not be a complete call if the divine Being does not acknowledge receipt of your *pra*. The *pra* and the *yer* added together is simply how we relate to the divine Being. Jesus Christ taught us how to pray the kingdom way in Matthew 6:9-13.

1. "Our Father in heaven, Hallowed be Your name" (v. 9). You are acknowledging that you do have a relationship with Him as you present **(P)** yourself, His child.
2. "Your kingdom come. Your will be done on earth as it is in heaven" (v. 10). You are requesting **(R)** that His will be done, giving up your will to yield to His.
3. "Give us this day our daily bread" (v. 11). You are not only asking, but you are aligning yourself to Him, as your Source, thus aligning **(A)** yourself to the Source of your blessings and supply.
4. "And forgive us our debts, as we forgive our debtors" (v. 12). This is a two-way deal; if you **(Y)** expect Him to answer you, forgive you

your debts/sins; you must be willing and ready
to forgive your debtors.

5. "And do not lead us into temptation, but deliver
us from the evil one" (v. 13). You are
expressing your dependency on Him, the
Effendi **(E)**, Greek for "Master," to keep you
from evil, from yielding to temptation; thus,
you are asking for His protection, for Him to
deliver you from the power of the evil one.

6. "For Yours is the kingdom and the power and
the glory forever. Amen" (v. 13). You are
giving Him thanks in advance because you
know He will respond **(R)**, He will answer your
prayer. If you put the bold letters together, you
have the word **"PRAYER."**

When you are in the Lord's presence in prayer,
before you make your requests, it is good to humbly:

1. **Present** yourself before the throne of grace.
2. **Render** praises and worship to Him.
3. **Align** yourself with Him; let Him enjoy your
presence in His presence.
4. **Yield** yourself to His will. Enjoy your intimacy
by making Him alone your ultimate focus.
5. **Expect** answers to your prayer.
6. **Render,** offer praises; give Him an upfront
praise for your healing, provision, blessing, and
miracles.

When you pray, your expressions of faith in
prayer on earth are converted into a spiritual wave
through the Spirit of God into a sweet-smelling savor
before the throne of grace, or before the **Effendi**. He is
the only One who is able to **respond** to your needs
anywhere, anytime, when no one else can. God
acknowledges the **receipt (R)** of your prayer **(pra)**.

You, in turn, will feel a release, peace, and joy in your heart once the burden is lifted. God will answer your prayer in accordance with His word, His will, and His timing, which is best for you. Sometimes God's response to your prayer may be instant or a little delayed. Other times, it may tarry for long, but never give up because delay is not denial.

A Brief History of Prayer

> And as for Seth, to him also a son was born; and he named him Enosh. Then men began to call on the name of the Lord [pray].
>
> Genesis 4:26

Enoch, son of Jared, was the first man to develop a serious relationship with God after the fall of mankind. He loved the Lord and was so intimate with God that God took him to heaven to be with Him. Enoch did not have to die to go to heaven to be with the Lord; the Lord, with whom all things are possible, just translated him into glory, bypassing the law of death.

> And Enoch walked with God; and he was not, for God took him.
>
> Genesis 5:24

Cain and Abel, his brother, were the first in Scripture to bring offerings to the Lord. They both built altars unto Him and offered their sacrifices upon the altars they built.

> And in the process of time it came to pass that **Cain brought an offering [gift] of the fruit of the ground to the**

Lord. Abel also brought of the firstborn of his flock and of their fat. And the Lord respected Abel and his offering.
> Genesis 4:3-4 (emphasis added)

Noah, the son of Lamech, was the third man to institute sacrificial worship. Noah loved the Lord and worshiped Him. He, too, built an altar unto the Lord, which represented worship, and offered sacrifices to God upon the altar he built in appreciation of the Lord for Noah's surviving the flood, because God spared him and his household.

Then Noah built an altar to the Lord, and took of every clean animal and of every clean bird, and **offered burnt offerings on the altar.**
> Genesis 8:20 (emphasis added)

After Noah, Abraham, the son of Terah, was called by God. Abraham practiced both worship and prayer as he offered his sacrifices to the Lord on the altar that he built.

Then the Lord appeared to Abram and said, "To your descendants I will give this land." And there he built an altar to the Lord, who had appeared to him. Then Abram moved his tent, and went and dwelt by the terebinth trees of Mamre, which are in Hebron, and built an altar there to the Lord.
> Genesis 12:7; 13:18

Abraham's Life Changed

The divine change in Abraham's life began after his encounter with Melchizedek. Melchizedek blessed him, and the blessing of Melchizedek brought Abraham to the limelight; thus, he found favor in the sight of God that literally changed his life, call, and ministry.

> Then Melchizedek king of Salem brought out bread and wine; he was the priest of God Most High. And he blessed him and said: "Blessed be Abram of God Most High, possessor of heaven and earth; and blessed be God Most High, who has delivered your enemies into your hand." And he gave him a tithe of all.
>
> Genesis 14:18-20

> After these things the word of the Lord came to Abram in a vision, saying, "Do not be afraid, Abram. I am your shield, your exceedingly great reward."
>
> Genesis 15:1

Abraham soon became a prayer intercessor for his relation Lot and his family (see Genesis 18:16-32).

Abraham's Servant Prayed

Abraham was not only prayerful; he taught his servants how to pray as well.

> Then the servant took ten of his master's camels and departed, for all his master's goods were in his hand. And he arose and went to

Mesopotamia, to the city of Nahor. And he made his camels kneel down outside the city by a well of water at evening time, the time when women go out to draw water. Then he said [prayed], "O Lord God of my master Abraham, please give me success this day, and show kindness to my master Abraham. Behold, here I stand by the well of water, and the daughters of the men of the city are coming out to draw water. Now let it be that the young woman to whom I say, 'Please let down your pitcher that I may drink,' and she says, 'Drink, and I will also give your camels a drink'—let her be the one You have appointed for Your servant Isaac. And by this I will know that You have shown kindness to my master."

Genesis 24:10-14

Prayer life experience: Never start praying until you can really believe God, until your heart is ready to submit and commune with God. Prayer is much more than just words or talking. Effective prayer must be born out of faith, sincerity, and a burden. The king's presence is not a place for unstable and faithless people. When you come before God in prayer, begin with faith, fellowship by faith, end by faith, and continue by faith.

Prayer Is Advancing Daily

Prayer is advancing daily in the lives of those that have given their lives to the prayer ministry. Prayer has not only advanced dramatically, but has grown relationally. Today we can come into God's presence with the fruits of our lips, with praise and thanksgiving. Yes, we can pass through the gates of praise, into His sanctuary, until we come face to face with the King of Kings and the Lord of Lords. It is indeed a breakthrough that we can relate to God through prayer, through the power of His Word, guided by His Spirit, without having to pass through any human priest or third party.

Chapter 3

Phone Versus Prayer

In the daily life of an average person in this technological age, the telephone, the cell phone, is becoming man's best friend. In the United States, for example, many people see their phone as their best companion. Cell phones are portable; you can take yours anywhere possible because you have developed a strong attachment to it. The attachment is so strong that you cannot afford to take its absence for granted.

As it is with your phone as a means of communication with man, so it should be with your prayer life as a means of communication with God. I have a question for you: How is your prayer life or your Bible study life? How strong is your relationship, your attachment, and your consecutiveness with the ministry of prayer and Bible study, compared with your relationship and attachment to your phone? God has commanded you and me to live a life of prayer—what are you doing about it?

> Then He spoke a parable to them, that men always ought to pray and not lose heart [not faint or give up]. . . . Rejoice always, pray without ceasing, in

everything give thanks; for this is the
will of God in Christ Jesus for you.
Luke 18:1; 1 Thessalonians 5:16-18

You willingly made the choice to sign a
contract to acquire your phone, just as you entered into
a covenant relationship with the Lord. The contract
you signed was voluntary, and it was you who chose to
go with the plan they offered or the one you wanted. I
am not talking about the pay-as-you-go type of phone.
Your phone service provider needed a commitment
from you to ensure that you know what you are
entering into. The terms and conditions, with which
you are expected to comply, paying your bills on time
as well as others, are clearly spelled out. Both the
provider's responsibilities and yours are in fine print in
the contract. The provider is under obligation to be
committed to you and to provide you the services for
which you are paying. If you break the contract before
it expires, your phone service provider will make you
pay penalties. If you are able to keep to the phone
contract, why is it a problem for you to keep to the
covenant terms in prayer with the Lord?

Prayer Connection
If you do not have a prayer line as you have a
phone line, I suggest you develop one. The starting
point, however, is your salvation—that is giving your
entire life over to Jesus Christ. It does not matter if you
were born in the church, or if your father is or was a
pastor, and that you go to church occasionally on
ceremonial days. Giving your life to Jesus Christ is a
personal thing and must be voluntary, just as your
phone contract was personal and voluntary. If you have
not given your life to Jesus, you do not have any place
in Him. Jesus Christ is our chief Shepherd; He will
only lead those who are part of His fold. Many people

will be surprised to find them-selves rejected on judgment day, not because they did not live a good life or go to church. But because they did not personally accept or receive Jesus Christ into their hearts and lives as their Lord and Savior, they will have no place in Him. Jesus Christ is the only way to eternal life and salvation. Accepting Him as your Lord and Savior is your passport to heaven.

Connect With Jesus

Everyone loves to be connected to family members, friends, and loved ones, but the best connection there is and will ever be is the connection to Life, Jesus Christ, the Author and the Finisher of our faith. The one and only way to connect to Jesus is simply by surrendering your life to Him. **"But as many as received Him"** [not as many as visited the church, or lived a good life outside the parameter of God's will, Word, and grace], **"to them He gave the right"** [the power and the privilege] **"to become children of God, to those who believe in His name"** (John 1:12, emphasis added).

It is a good thing to go to church, and it is great to live a good life, but only those who *received* Jesus Christ as Lord and Savior did He give the right to become God's children.

> **Jesus said to him: "I am the way, the truth, and the life. No one comes to the Father except through Me."**
> John 14:6

> **Nor is there salvation in any other, for there is no other name under heaven given among men by which we must be saved.**
> Acts 4:12

The Jesus Network

As children of God, we are all members of one body, called the body of Christ. The body of Christ is the network of Jesus Christ. If you are not part of the network of Jesus Christ, your line may not go through when you call heaven. Your prayer line will not be turned down or rejected; it simply will be redirected to heaven's customer service center, where you will be asked to sign up with Jesus Christ first, before your prayer connection can gain access into God's network. So if you are not yet a child of God, even though you may be going to church, you really need to give your life to Jesus Christ now. Get signed up today, and you will have a direct line to the throne of heaven right away. There is no waiting period.

Do you need direction for your life, or seek new possibilities in life? Get connected to Jesus. Being connected to Jesus is the start or the turning point that sets you on your path to eternal life. I am not saying if you connect to Jesus Christ today, all your problems will be solved. All I am saying is that as you allow Him to do His perfect work in you and through you; He will deliver you from them all. You still may face or have problems on your path to glory, but He will see you through every step of the way, until you become victorious. Put your trust totally in Him, let Him have His way in you and through you, and your life will never be the same again. I do know for sure that with God, all things are possible, and I know for sure that there is nothing too hard for the Lord to handle or do.

Prayer life experience: You must be prayerful to be able to overcome the intense current opposition or the wind of Satan's opposition and have a breakthrough. You must never let your guard down. You overcome evil daily to get to the next level in your relationship with God without burning out. The power of prayer helps us find grace for help in times of need.

The oil of joy that flows from your prayer life experience (sessions) will bring refreshment from the presence of the Lord to your soul and keep you encouraged to press on to the mark of His high calling upon your life.

Get Connected to a Bible-Believing Church

After signing up, or giving your life to Jesus Christ, find a Bible-believing church in your area where the Word of God is preached without compromise, and get connected to the church of the living God. Become a part of Jesus' network as members of the body of Christ. Learn under the pastor all you need to know about prayer. Let Him and His ministers help you configure, or program, your prayer line, just as you had to configure, or program, your new phone. After the configuration, you do not need to wait to start using your prayer line; you can start right away after you sign up, by giving your life over to Jesus Christ.

Prayer life experience: Now that you are a child of God, start enjoying your prayer line. Please pray on good days the same way you will pray on bad days. Not praying on good days will invite, or make room for, bad days in your new life experience. Do not wait for bad days to come around before you start praying; it may be too late then. Moreover, you may become too confused to pray, as there will be too many distractions and alternatives. There is no genuine heartfelt prayer that is a waste. Your prayer is a seed; water it with your faith and love, for faith operates by love. It is better to store up prayers than not to pray at all for the angels of God to tap on your behalf in the day of trouble.

Relationship and Prayer

Giving your life to Jesus Christ will not automatically make you a faithful warrior for Christ. You must learn to walk by faith to be able to apply the principles of faith in order to grow from faith to faith. When it comes to prayer, you must have a firm personal relationship with God to have a sure prayer connection. Relationship with God is different from just acknowledging what you have been told about Him. You just have to know Him for yourself and develop a passionate, intimate relationship with Him.

You can walk to any local dealer you prefer today to buy your handset, just as you can walk to any church or denomination you prefer to give your life to Jesus Christ. Simply buying a handset will not get you connected to any phone service provider's network; you must sign up. The same process is applicable to your prayer connection. Giving your life to Jesus is step one, developing a personal intimate relationship with God is step two, and it goes on and on from there until you get to heaven.

Prayer life experience: When people mock you, rejoice. Never put your head down; you serve a living God. He is the same yesterday, today, and forever. If God did not let the men of old down, He will not let you down. If you can only be patient, very soon the same people mocking you now, while you are going through painful circumstances, will join you to sing hosanna. It is only through patience that your faith can be made perfect, and when your faith is perfected, you can boldly say, **"I know that my Redeemer lives"** (Job 19:25). You will soon begin to sing, "See what the Lord has done."

Prepaid Phone

Many people prefer to use prepaid phones as opposed to regular contract phones. Similarly, many Christians today treat their relationship with God as they do their prepaid phones. Because they do not want responsibility, they go prepaid with God. For example, if they do not like it in one local church, they will switch their connection to another local church because they are not on a contract. The majority of us are serving God because of what He can do for us, not because of who He is. Some people are miracle-seekers, and those who are not just want to belong somehow. Some people go to church not because they want intimate relationship with Him, but because it is a nice thing to do every Sunday, according to Mama and Daddy, or Grandma and Grandpa. To some people, it is simply a "look at me being good" game.

Pay as You Go

Paying as you go is a new way of prepaying for phone services. Some Christians also do this with God. They want to live their Christian lives the way they choose, not the way God chooses. These "pay-as-you-go" Christians do not like to be told the truth, corrected, or rebuked when they are wrong. If you correct "pay-as-you-go" Christians, they think you are jealous. When they are rebuked, they will just switch, and are connected to another local church the next Sunday. They go to the church where they will be lost in the crowd, unfruitful, unfaithful, and without responsibilities. Most "pay-as-you-go" Christians do not grow spiritually. They long for more of themselves and less of God. They are comfortable where they are. They just come to church, and after church, they are gone with the wind until the following Sunday. They hate to be told to take up any responsibility in the house of God because it will take away some of their fun time. They have one uncompromising policy: They do whatever they want, how they want, and you do it their way. If you do not buy their policy or take to their ungodly advice, they get angry, disconnect themselves from you, and move from one local church to another.

Chapter 4

Church Prostitution

The "pay-as-you-go" Christian deception system in the body of Christ is taking a deep root, and the gravity of its careless nature is turning many Christians into church "prostitutes." (When I say prostitute, I am not talking about sexual misconduct; I am simply talking about those who are not able to commit to one local church for long). Even though some of the "pay-as-you-go" Christians seem to love the Lord, their instability and insecurity are a problem and risk to new converts who might want to follow their careless, irresponsible, and unstable nature. The "pay-as-you-go" system in the church has changed a lot of people, turned them into church harlots, to the extent that the people who ought to be a blessing to the local church God has placed them in by becoming church builders have turned themselves into church destroyers and church breakers.

They split the church of God (break away, as they call it) because they do not want to submit. If you cannot submit to the authority God has placed you under, who will submit to you? The devil is sitting in the corner of the entrance to the church, laughing and making some church leaders today operate under a curse. God is busy building His church, and we, His children, are busy tearing it down with our pride, disobedience, and insubordination to God's authorities—the leaders God has placed over us as pastors, teachers, apostles, prophets, and evangelists.

Your Local Church

If your local church cannot change you, you can change or transform your local church with prayer. Stand in the gap, fast, and pray until God sends down revival to that local church. Do not leave the local church because the pastor does not take your advice; leave only when God tells you to. Let it be that for your sake, God will spare that church and will not destroy it, but will purge it and pour grace into it. Who knows if that is the very reason God sent you to that local church—to help those who attend connect with God as they ought to. I am sure if there was no need (i.e., a task or mission for you to accomplish) for you to meet at the local church where you are, God would not have sent you there. Who knows if what you are complaining about is what God sent you there to fix. God wants to use you to fix the problem. Let Him use you; do not run away from it. Who knows if you are the answer to their prayer, the Joshua God wants to use to bring the change needed when their Moses has failed them in that very area. Please, let God use you to move that local church to its next phase!

Prayer life experience: While you are enjoying the comforts of life, do not take prayer for granted because if Satan finds any opportunity to hurt or kill you, he will gladly do it and move on. Prayer keeps you from evil and will keep you alive by the grace of God. In fact, start praying now that you are comfortable to keep evil away from you, and pray always, as long as you have the breath of God in you, for there is no prayer after death. You will not be able to say amen to any prayer said over you in the grave. Amen is for the living, not the dead.

If You Must Leave Any Church

If you must leave one church for another, please do not cause problems before leaving. You must not leave amid quarreling, anger, bitterness, and unforgiveness. I wonder what kind of church you can raise with the very nature and fruits of the devil in the house of God. Is it not the same house about which the Lord has said, **"My house shall be called a house of prayer for all people."** How are you able to pray with bitterness, anger, hatred, and unforgiveness stored in your heart against your fellow Christians? I pray that the Lord will have mercy and help us, especially us church leaders, because we will all give an account to God about how we nurture and cater to His sheep that He has placed in our care.

Numerical Strength

The church of God is not about numerical strength in a single church or a big sanctuary, as every church leader would love it to be. The church of God is much more than that. It is about connecting people with God and ensuring that they stay connected to God for life. I have seen big, medium-sized, and small churches with beautiful buildings filled to the brim without God's presence in them. Having a large membership is good, but that should never be your driving force. The Spirit of God should be your driving force, not numbers. The Lord has said, **"I will build my church."** You and I cannot grow, or build, the church of God, for without Him, we can do nothing.

We can follow five or ten steps, or principles, of church growth to attract people, but without the Spirit of God in us and in all we are doing, it is vanity. You can have an organized, high-definition, mechanized religion, and fun and rosy activities, which may attract people to your church building, but they do not attract people to God. In your congregation, how many of the people are passionately committed or intimately connected to Jesus Christ? Operating your ministry under a combined anointing is great, but wait until you face your fear alone.

The ministry of Jesus Christ was not about numbers. He came to redeem, restore, and reconnect us to God. For Him to succeed in His mission on earth, His prayer line was always open and firmly connected to God. He had to pray through to have a breakthrough in His life and ministry here on earth. If you are not doing the above [prayerful] as a minister of God, you need to go back to Bethel, to PRAY and reevaluate your calling and mission from God. You can have the biggest church in the world, work miracles and still be unfulfilled before the Lord our God, though the world will think you've got it good here on earth. What is God's report about you? Remember, He is the judge, not the children of men. How many people among your church members will make it to heaven if Jesus comes today? Please, prayerfully think about this matter.

Man or Woman of God, Fear God

The saddest thing of all is that you can have the best, fast-growing church and still go to hell. God's work and calling are about doing it right as led by the Spirit of God, and doing it God's way with a humble heart. Dear man or woman of God, fear God so the devil can fear you, or become a friend of the devil by operating in the flesh, in the counsel of men, and lose the [fear] respect of God. Some of our church leaders today love the cares of this life and its glory more than the glory of God. The glory of God comes only by holy living, obedience, humility and by prayer.

If Jesus Christ shows up in the air right now, what is your stand—what will He say to you, servant of God? Are you into the business of church ministry for the money or for the mission? Money is good, but that is not why my Jesus came [He did not call you to money; He called you to Himself, to serve Him and His people]. He came to save souls, not to milk them of their resources and take advantage of them, as some church leaders do today, especially in some of our television ministries. I am not against television ministries, nor am I against giving money. It is good to give, I give too. But I am against putting money before the cross or putting my Jesus' anointing and healing for sale.

Prayer life experience: Do you know that the God of the valley is also the God of the mountain, the God of the rich is also the God of the poor, and the God of those that are rejoicing is the same God of those that may be mourning? He will make all things beautiful for you in His time if you can patiently wait on Him and not give heed to the drawing of the flesh. Remember, my friend, they that wait upon God, according to the Word of God, shall be like Mount Zion, which shall never be moved. Please be patient. Learn to wait on God. He is always on time and certainly will not fail if your faith, courage, and heart doubt not. Do not allow anyone to turn you into a mini-god. It is a fearful thing to be caught daring to share God's glory.

Contract and Covenant

When you sign a contract with your phone service provider, the contract is binding for both parties. When you sign up for, or give your life to, Jesus Christ, you come into a covenant relationship with God. Signing your phone contract automatically makes you responsible to your phone service provider, although how you use your phone is totally up to you., Your covenant with God is the same, from the day you sign up for, or give your life over to, Jesus Christ. God is not asking for too much from us. All God is asking for is that you and I keep our part of the covenant. How you live or maintain your Christian life is totally up to you. God gave you a will, and it is your choice to be faithful, or not to be unfaithful, to Him. That is why God told us in His Word that it is up to us to work out our salvation with fear and trembling, which, of course, is the reason why you and I will give account to God on how we lived our lives here on earth.

Your phone connection company, or service provider, will not force any contract on you if you do not want to sign up with that provider, will it? Neither is God going to force you to obey Him. Jesus Christ did not force you to sign up for, or give your life to, Him; you chose to be connected to Him. My friend, there is no commitment without a responsibility. If you say you are committed to something but do not have any responsibilities that propel your commitment, you are not committed to anything yet. It is very easy to say, "I do," but it is not always easy to pay the price till the very end. Now that you are connected to God, why are you not serving Him with all sincerity and faithfulness? After signing up for your phone, you now have a responsibility, which, of course, states you must make payment for your phone every month. How do you get your money? You get your money by working, by doing something. You labor; you sweat. Your sweat comes directly or indirectly from your blood, and your blood is your life. If you can connect your phone with your life, why can't you connect God with your life?

God Is a Covenant-Keeping God

God is a covenant-keeping God. Are you keeping your part of your covenant with Him? Your phone service provider can only keep to its part of the contract when it can. Your phone service provider was made by God, and its services to you can be limited by light, weather, and environmental instabilities. God is unlimited and can limit anything and anyone if He so desires. When you choose to sign up for Jesus Christ, please do all you can to live for Him. The road to glory may not be rosy all the time, but it is sure, for the prepared—those who are determined and sold out for God. "My grace is sufficient for you" is the promise we embrace from God, and our own promise to Him is to never look back, give up, or quit.

Prayer life experience: God will not deny Himself. He cannot deny His Word, and He is under obligation to bring His Word to pass. Are you committed to your word, your commitment and promises you have made to God? God will always keep His part of the covenant. He expects you and me to keep our part of the covenant by remaining faithful and obedient to His Word through prayer and evangelism.

God Rewards Faithfulness

God can turn His back on love when it comes in conflict with our sin or the flesh, but He cannot turn his back on His covenant and principles. God is love. He is just and never partial. That is why He sometimes may appear cruel to us the way He does things or the kinds of things He allows to happen to His loved ones. Jesus Christ is God's love. On the cross He bore our sins. God turned His back on His love so His principle and covenant would not be compromised. Does that mean God did not love Jesus? No, that means He is God. He cannot compromise His covenant and principle for anyone. He is no respecter of persons. Our God is the God of justice. If you have faith and have no works, you are just like the people of the world, even if you claim to be a follower of Jesus Christ. If you are a prayer machine and do not live a clean life, you are like a sign, which directs people to places, yet itself goes nowhere. God answers prayers, but only rewards faithfulness.

> By faith Enoch was taken away so that he did not see death, "and was not found, because God had taken him"; for before he was taken he had this testimony, that he pleased God.
> But without faith it is impossible to please Him, for he who comes to God must believe that He is, and that He is a rewarder of those who diligently seek Him.
>
> Hebrews 11:5-6

Please do not tell me you are full of faith when you are not faithful to God, or that you are filled with the Holy Spirit, who is the Spirit of truth, and you do not speak the truth or live a life of truth. There is no sitting on the fence with God, with one leg in the church, and the other in the world. You must belong to one because you cannot serve two masters.

The Manufacturer's Manual

When you got your phone, its manufacturer gave you instructions in the manufacturer's handbook, telling you in writing how to use your cell phone, so you can make the best use of your investment. If you ignore the manufacturer's instructions and try to manipulate the product as you choose, then run into problems and call the manufacturer for support, you will be on your own because you did not follow the manufacturer's instructions. If you abuse your phone, the manufacturer is not liable for any malfunction or damages. You may not get a refund or replacement.

Prayer life experience: If you were patient enough to fast and pray, you will be patient enough to trust and obey. The very day you lose your faith and fail to trust in God, the birds of the air will feed on your miracles. Do not give up or quit. Delay never means denial; rather, rely and feed on God's faithfulness daily. If you could do the impossible or work miracles yourself, why did you pray to God? If you listen to Satan's deception or the unbelief of men and doubt God, what can they do to help you?

My friend, vain is the help of men and Satan. It is only God that is well able to do all things. Hold on, endure now, wait on the Lord, refuse to doubt or quit today, and you will rejoice tomorrow. God's ways and His timing are always the best for us.

Chapter 5

Prayer and Phone Connections

As your phone requires connection through a service provider, so your prayer line requires the service of the Holy Spirit. You must connect to Him if you are to have a good relationship with Him. That is the reason our God, our Maker, gave you the Bible. The Bible is His manufacturer's manual. Do you read and study the Bible, your life manual?

All Scripture is given by inspiration of God, and is profitable for doctrine, for reproof, for correction, for instruction in righteousness, that the man of God may be complete, thoroughly equipped for every good work. Be diligent to present yourself approved to God, a worker who does not need to be ashamed, rightly dividing the word of truth. Nevertheless the solid foundation of God stands, having this seal: "The Lord knows those who are His," and, "Let everyone who names the name of Christ depart from iniquity [sin]." But in a great house, there are not only vessels of gold and silver, but also of wood and clay, some for honor and some for dishonor. Therefore if anyone cleanses himself from the latter [sin and self], he will be a vessel for honor, sanctified and useful for the Master, prepared for every good work.

2 Timothy 3:16-17; 2:15, 19-21

I pray that your phone, the Internet, and games will not become a thorn in your prayer life and relationship with God.

Children of God

It is a great privilege that you and I can interact with God in the place of prayer, but it is a sad thing to note that we prefer to play rather than pray—forgetting that bodily exercise profits little. Prayer can move mountains; its accomplishments and benefits can last a lifetime. It is okay to talk to men for men, but it is greater to talk to God for men. Men can sympathize or empathize with you as they have the opportunity to do so in your times of trouble, but only God has the answers. He is our present help in times of trouble, the peace we have in the midst of the storms of life. God has said **"Fear not. . . . I will help you"** (Isaiah 41:10). Therefore, believe in God and believe in the power of your prayer.

Stop building your confidence and reliance on men, for vain is the help of man. No human being will be able to help you move to your next level unless the Lord moves upon his or her heart to do so. Stop relying on man-made gods, demonic powers, and other powers that people rely on. They have power, but their power is powerless before our Most High God. Only the living God truly loves us unconditionally, and He is passionately committed to loving us for all eternity. Our God is the only God in the universe, who came down to us (humanity), to identify with us. He came to reconcile us to Himself. People seek other gods, but our God came down to earth to seek us. Truly and surely, God's love for us is amazing.

Your Phone Use Is Your Choice

Just because you have a cell phone and do not want to use it to call others for any reason does not mean people will not call you if they want to. The exception is if you place your phone number on the National Do Not Call Registry (in the United States). However, your phone service provider will not waive your monthly payment because you decided not to make use of your phone. You placed yourself under obligation to pay for the service the moment you signed up for it, whether you use it or not. You can decide to keep it off, not pick up calls; it is up to you.

Prayer Is a Choice

Just because God saved you and appointed you for service does not mean trouble will not come knocking at your door. As long as we live in this world, we will not be problem- or temptation-free until we attain the fullness of Christ. If you are not in connection with God, you are connected to your flesh (yourself) or the devil. Every one of us at one time or another is connected to somebody or to something. For example, I met a sister a long time ago who was trusting God for a husband. Five years passed, and no potential husband emerged. So I asked her, "Sister, have you prayed?" She responded, "Pray?" I said, "Yes." She told me, "God knows I need a husband, and in His own time, He will give me one." I told her, "If you do not pray, you may have to wait for another five years before you learn how to ASK in prayer." She suddenly became very spiritual and started quoting Scriptures to me, trying to prove her point. I shared with her the revelation about the power of prayer, but she did not believe. She was only twenty-five years old then. What I told her at that time ended up happening.

She learned to pray the tenth year after my encounter with her, and that same year, she got married, at the age of thirty-five.

Nothing moves until you speak to it, and no one will answer your call until you call. Heaven will not act until you pray. Only Satan comes in uninvited because he is a thief. Satan will not stop stealing from you until you take your stand in the place of prayer and tell him, "Enough is enough." The choice is yours; use it or lose it. God has set principles for prayer. He will not go against His principles, even though He can still change His mind as He wills. That is why only He has the power to kill and make alive without any questions asked. God has said in His Word, **"Ask, and it will be given to you; seek, and you will find; knock, and it will be opened to you"** (Matthew 7:7). Let us study this verse of Scripture systematically, briefly.

"Ask, and It Will Be Given to You"

If you claim you believe in God, in His power and ability, why are you shying away from prayer? The starting point is for you to recognize the fact that God is real and well capable of accomplishing what He says He will do. The principle of asking gives us confidence and assurance that He is our Source. We ask because He loves us and we love Him. God knows what you need, He really does, but He wants you to put your faith to work. If your faith is not expressed, then it will not glorify Him. Anything done without faith is a sin, and God will not be a part of it.

> **But without faith it is impossible to please Him, for he who comes to God must believe that He is, and that He is a rewarder of those who diligently seek Him.**
>
> Hebrews 11:6

Whatever is not from faith is sin.
Romans 14:23c

Now the just shall live by faith; but if anyone draws back, My soul [God speaking of Himself] has no pleasure in him [or her].
Hebrews 10:38

"Seek, and You Will Find"

If you have prayed in faith because you believed in God's faithfulness, then act upon what you claim to believe He is able to do. Exercise your faith, and put your faith to work. Confessing faith is one thing, and exercising faith (taking action) is another.

But do you want to know, O foolish man, that faith without works is dead? Was not Abraham our father justified by works when he offered Isaac his son on the altar? Do you see that faith was working together with his works, and by works [action] faith was made perfect?
James 2:20-22

It is like a man who claims to have prayed for a job and will not go to apply for any. There was a man named Cruz. Cruz loved the Lord very much and did all he could to live right with God. His life was a testimony to all the people who knew him, and he knew his Bible well. It happened that in time, a very bad storm hit the village. The storm busted out of heaven with a lot of heavy rain, resulting in a huge flood. The flood pounded Cruz's house hard. He prayed all the ways he knew how to pray and quoted the Scriptures. He called upon the God of his salvation for help and deliverance.

The situation became so bad that if help did not arrive quickly, Cruz was going to die. The more the flood intensified, the more Cruz prayed. God heard his prayers and sent him help. Rescuers came in with a boat to save him, but he refused to get in the boat. After a while, the water was almost covering him. He was still praying, calling on God to come down and save him. God made it possible for another rescue team to see him from a helicopter. They let down a rope for him to hold onto so they could pull him out of the flood. He still refused. In his ignorance, he believed his faith was so strong that God would appear to save him. He refused to give up and continued quoting Scriptures. "My God, You promised to save me. Even though I pass through the fire, I will not be burnt. If I go through the waters, I will not sink, for the Lord is with me." Cruz refused the help from the rescuers, and he died.

When Cruz got to heaven, he asked God, "Father, You knew how much I loved You and trusted You. Lord, I served You faithfully—why did You fail me?" God told him, "Cruz, my son, I am a faithful God, and I take delight in my faithfulness. Forever my word is settled and will not fail. Cruz, my child, I did not fail you; you had zeal, but lacked knowledge, wisdom, and discernment. I was the One who sent those rescuers to help you out when the flood came to you. First, I sent you the lifeboat, but you refused to get in it. Then I sent you the lifeline from the helicopter, but you refused to line up. You failed yourself for your lack of knowledge, wisdom, and discernment." He had to ask God to forgive him for his ignorance. Are you like Cruz? I hope you learn this good lesson.

Some of us are bent on doing things our way or expecting God to do things our way, and have lost a lot of battles, blessings, and even souls to Satan, the devil. Why do you not let God have His way? You just cast all your cares upon Him in prayer, and let Him take it from there. Some of your prayers were answered the very first time or day you prayed, but for a lack of knowledge, wisdom, and discernment, you were not sensitive to the movement of the Spirit of God. So a lot of answered prayers and blessings are hanging in the air while you are still expecting God to answer them.

In the book of Acts of the apostles chapter twelve, the church prayed intensely for Peter to be delivered from prison and from death. God answered the church's prayer and sent down an angel from heaven to deliver Peter. Peter was delivered and came to the place where prayers were being said for his deliverance. He knocked on the door and was greeted by a little girl where the church was still busy praying for what God had already done. When they were told that Peter was at the door, they did not believe it. Many prayers have been answered, but because of the lack of discernment, some of us are still praying over and over for the same thing every day.

Prayer point: Pray that the Lord will open your spiritual eyes that you might be able to see beyond the natural world. Pray that God will give you an ear to hear when He speaks, and that the Lord will give unto you the Spirit of discernment for you to know that they that are with us (angels of God) are more than the evil hosts of Satan, in Jesus' name.

Chapter 6

Prayer, Faith, and Action

Anytime you pray by faith, you pray because you believe in the power of prayer. You pray because you know that with God all things are possible, I suppose. What stops you from knocking on the doors to men's hearts, company and government doors, or whatever doors you are trusting God to open for you by the same faith with which you have prayed? If your prayer can move heaven, heaven will move men on your behalf, causing all things to work together for your good. If the seed of your prayer was planted by faith through your asking, you will have to water your prayer seed with the same faith, add some patience by the water of the Word of God, and when it is time for harvest, put your faith to work by reaching out to dare the impossible.

If you prayed for a job, act upon your faith and go to apply for a job. If they call you for an interview, go for the interview, and if God says it is yours, it will surely be yours. Go to the interview by faith, and expect to get the job by faith. God has answered your prayers and has opened doors for you. All you need to do is walk in and possess your possession. You must get rid of doubt, complaining, murmuring, worries, and fear to be able to take hold of your possession.

Prayer life experience: It is time for us to be commanding communicators as far as prayer is concerned, because nothing moves until you speak to it. You may not experience the manifestations of the Spirit of God until you step out by faith, confessing the miraculous, envisioning the miraculous, expecting to see the miraculous, and then doing the miraculous to the glory of God. Give it a trial this week, and see God prove Himself strong on your behalf.

Have Faith in God

Jesus answered and said to them, "Have faith in God. For assuredly, I say to you, whoever says to this mountain, 'Be removed and be cast into the sea,' and does not doubt in his heart, but believes that those things he says will be done, he will have whatever he says. Therefore I say to you, whatever things you ask when you pray, believe that you receive them, and you will have them."

Mark 11:22-24

Until now you have asked nothing in My name [even though you just believe and I know you do]. Ask [says Jesus; if you do not ask, you may not receive, no matter how expectant you might be, but if you ask], you will receive, that your joy may be full.

John 16:24

But let him ask in faith, with no doubting, for he who doubts is like a wave of the sea driven and tossed by the wind. For let not that man suppose that he will receive anything from the

Lord; he is a double-minded man, unstable in all his ways.

James 1:6-8

Are You Proud of Your Phone?

Almost everyone is proud of his phone, especially people who have the ones introduced most recently to the market. Right from the day you got your new phone, it made you proud; you were not ashamed to publicly shine and show up with your newly acquired phone. When you wanted to make calls or receive calls, you did it with elegance.

How Is Your Attitude Toward Prayer?

Since the day you knew how to pray, how is your prayer experience progressing and growing? Do you openly pray in public places? Do you read your Bible in public, or can you even boldly say you are a Christian in public? You can use your cell phone anywhere—at home, on the street, in your car, on the train, on a ship, on an airplane, at school, while shopping, and at work—but can you do the same with prayer? If you cannot, something is wrong. Check your life. It is time for you to take your stand, as the apostles of old did in their day.

The Word of God and prayer are being put out of schools and offices. The name of God is attacked, mocked, and reduced by the media without fear, respect, and reverence. Yet our church leaders are sitting around watching television, engulfed with the spirit of the Internet, playing games on the computer, or busy on the phone preparing for the next big activity or event, how the church will bring in more money, not more souls to the kingdom of God. Our church leaders, church fathers, and everyone that names the name of the Lord must take a stand if we do not want the powers of darkness to prevail over our earthly human governments, culture, and society, so that the devil cannot use the government and the socialist society to hinder the rights and privileges of the church of God. I strongly believe we can move our nations and governments toward God if we can agree in prayer. You can complain about your country's government all you want, but it will not change until you pray. God does not listen to complaints; He listens to and answers prayers.

Protecting Your Phone

The day you got your phone, you began to take responsibility for it. You are careful where you place it and do all you can to protect it from harm. You try to keep it from being stolen. Sometimes it seems you are more relational to your phone than to humanity because of the way you cherish your phone. It is always by your side and in sight so it will be readily available for you to pick up if someone calls.

Your Prayer

Do you protect and watch over your prayer life the same way you protect and watch over your phone? Do you take personal responsibility for your prayerlessness, or do you make excuses? Are you very concerned about your spiritual life, your Bible study life, and the kind of things you do as a representative of the one and only true God? God loved you so much, He saved you. God created you intelligent by giving you a will; you decide what you do, where you go. How you lead your life is completely your responsibility. If you love your phone, you protect your phone so you do not miss your calls, lose it, or damage it. Why, then, do you neglect your spiritual well-being? Which is greater, your phone or your spiritual well-being?

Protect Your Prayer Life

I have noticed that most of us children of God who have a phone always watch out for it to ring—but not every one of us watches in prayer. We care so much about our phones. How much do we care about our spiritual growth? For example, do you evangelize? Do you support your pastors and ministers to see to it that the work of the Lord prospers? Do you protect your pastor, ministers, and leaders when the busybodies in the church come around to gossip? Every child of God has a calling. God did not save or call anyone to just sit around and do nothing, so get up and do something. Live a life well pleasing to God. A sinful heart cannot produce a good aroma of prayer before the throne of God. What kind of smell does your prayer bring before the throne of grace? Can God freely ride on the wings of your prayer, or will He turn His back to it because it is polluted with hatred, bitterness, and unforgiveness toward your fellow man? Do you know that sometimes self and sin can contaminate your prayers and even the offerings made to God?

Prayer life experience: Let us be zealous for the Lord and guide our prayer life jealously for the Lord as a woman guides her man jealously, not wanting to see the glory of her privacy with another. Let us stop sharing God's glory with other things or persons in our lives, so we do not provoke the anger of God.

Your Phone Number

When you signed up for your phone, your telephone service provider gave you the phone number available. You did not give orders as to the numbers you must have because it was not in your power to do so, except if you were willing to pay extra money or if it was part of the package. The phone service provider gave you your phone numbers based on availability, which means he or she is in charge, not you. Also know that you rented the numbers from him or her, even though your handset or headset is yours to keep. This is because the same numbers you treasure today can become someone else's quickly if you fail to make payments.

Your Prayer

When you are called for prayer meetings or night vigils, do you attend? In your local church, are you humble enough to do any work your pastor wants you to do? God will not use or bless those He cannot lead. God's work is not and will never be optional. It is our responsibility as members of our local assemblies to do—not just the pastors' alone. We are supposed to be a team doing everything in love and in the bond of peace as the Spirit leads to the glory of God. God did not place you in the local church where you are now by accident. He brought you there because of the need in that house—so you can meet it—whether through labor, time, money, or ministry. Some people do not want to make God's work and His need a priority, but they want God to make their businesses, needs, and concerns a priority. Let us hear what Jesus, our example, has to say:

> "I must work the works of Him who sent Me while it is day; the night is coming when no one can work. As long as I am in the world [you in your local church, in your neighborhood], I am the light of the world." So Jesus said to them again, "Peace to you! As the Father has sent Me, I also send you."
>
> John 9:4-5; 20:21

Remember the word that I said to you, "A servant is not greater than his master."

John 15:20a

They are not of the world, just as I am not of the world. Sanctify them by Your truth. Your word is truth. As You sent Me into the world, I also have sent them into the world.

John 17:16-18

Chapter 7

Phone and Prayer Features (Part One)

Your phone has amazing features, and the more technology advances, the more new features are added. Your phone's manufacturer knows how to milk you (financially) carefully, seasonally, and wisely. Through its media and other advertisement strategies, the manufacturer makes you go wild by subjecting you to the burden of your soul's desires that will not move you toward God. You spend a lot of money to enhance, improve, and upgrade your device to communicate with the children of men.

Your Prayer Life

Similarly, your prayer life ought to advance as you grow from grace to grace, pressing for the mark of the high calling of God, not declining. Many of us are passionately pursuing and seeking alternative ways to replay our fervency for the Lord with fantasies and capitalistic ideals that will please us; activities that will bond us together in the flesh, but not bond us to or conform to the image of Jesus Christ. The Word of God, worship and prayer have little or no place when we gather. Today we have many capitalist, socialist pastors (orators and entertainers, not ministers), pastors and church leaders who do not care how you live your life or are not passionate about your spiritual growth as long as the money is coming in. A Christian brother told me how his local church elders tried to replace their midweek Bible studies with movies. It saddened my heart when I heard it. I went home to cry unto God on behalf of that church and its backsliding elders. My concern was that if one local church planted this evil seed in the soil of the body of Christ, it would begin to spread like wildfire, and before you know it, other churches already would have bought into it. What people dare not do in the Islamic fellowship or services is what the church of God wants to mess with. Where is the fear of God? Godly movies are not bad to watch, but they are no replacement for the Word of God or prayer. Jesus Christ overturned tables once in the temple during His earthly ministry. If we are not careful, God will start calling some of our church leaders home to heaven very soon, before they lead others astray. I will not be surprised to see the hand of God writing on the wall like in the days of Daniel. The temple of God ought to be the house of prayer, as it was in biblical times.

The Temple was turned into a den of thieves at the time Jesus overturned the tables of those who turned the house of God into business centers. Today many churches operate solely for money, not for the Great Commission. If you cannot trade your regular phone for a toy phone, why would you trade God's time, God's Word, for movies that will not empower you for the Great Commission or for active duty in God's service? The revival we are trusting God for may not come from Hollywood, from the movies, or through the media. Revival will only come when we passionately give ourselves to the ministry of prayer, to love, and to the drawing of the Spirit of God. Phones need a continual power source or supply to operate any of their functions. You need the correct batteries or amount of electricity to charge the battery. In a similar way, your Christian life needs a continual power source or supply by your constant connection with God through your prayer line and Bible studies. There are no substitutes.

Your Cell Phone Is Wireless

Your phone can transmit your words electronically and wirelessly into electronic waves and back into words. Nowadays, you can almost call anywhere you want with your phone, whether locally, nationally, or internationally. Technology is advancing; new wireless phone devices and accessories are introduced to the marketplace almost every quarter. Upgrades and enhanced accessories are available with hot and spicy features, as they make it sound in the advertisements of the latest features.

Your Prayer Line

Your prayer line has the ability to transmit your words, even the whispers of your heart. Those words you cannot share with any human being because people will not understand the cry of your innermost being. Such intimate words that you can only express to God during hard times, dark days, when you have no one else to look or turn to but God. I have been there so many times, and I have good news for you. God is still very faithful. He will not turn you down, nor will He let you down, if you can let go and let Him. Cast all your cares upon Him in the place of prayer and leave them there. He is abundantly able to do much more than we think or could ever imagine.

Your Phone Connection is Limited

There is no distance in the Spirit. You can supplicate for anyone anywhere in the world, and your prayer line can connect him or her to God wherever that person is. Sometimes I try to call Africa, but am unable to get through. The response messages are like, "All circuits are busy; please call again." This means our phone connection is limited. At times, phones drop calls (we get disconnected) and do not work (connect) in very remote places. Your phone line is limited to the earthly realm. Its connectivity could be obstructed by weather or electronic interferences. Your prayer line can connect to (move the hands of God on behalf of) anyone anywhere, to the high heavens. Just dial J-E-S-U-S, and you will hear Jesus say, "Hello, this is Jesus. How may I help you?" Tell Him all your doubts. Ask freely and sincerely. This process is thought-activated and faith-promoted. God's prayer line is safe, confidential, and secure. The government cannot eavesdrop without your concurrence. The sad thing is that the church of God is not accelerating in prayer the way technology is accelerating.

So many Christians today have more dependence on doctors, pharmacists, and medication than they do on the healing power of God through the power of prayer and the faithfulness of God. Please do not get me wrong, doctors are good, pharmacists and medications are great, but still it is God alone who can permanently heal. Doctors and medications are attainable to assist us—they are just means to our healing. Only God heals. Do not put all your trust and faith in medications or man-made machines because they can fail. Our God is the only One who is perfect and fails not. Take your medications as instructed by your medical care provider, but trust God for your healing, because physicians and pharmaceutical experts have no answers to many medical problems. Doubtless and compassionate faith conceived prayers prayed with all fervency and compassion have made a lot of difference in so many instances of healing where medications, doctors, and pharmaceutical experts failed. Such healing and divine intervention could not be illustrated, but have only one harmonious word of expression: "miracles."

Believe in Your Prayers

Again, only God fails not. Have faith in God because He alone has the final say in your affairs and situations. I just believe it is not over yet, until God says it is over. Doctors are human and do die; God is a Spirit and will never die. Believe in the power of God's infallible Word and believe also in the power of prayers. When you lack faith, feel confused, and do not know what else to do, put on the garment of praise and just praise on. If you really praise the Lord from your heart, God will ride on the wings of your praise to make the impossible possible in your life. Do not put your head down anymore. Do not be dejected, depressed, or weary, or cry as one without hope. Our God is not dead. Because He lives, you can face tomorrow. The Egyptians you see today (whatever you are going through today) you will see no more if you can honestly, fervently, and humbly pray, praise, and not doubt the faithfulness of God. God instructed Elijah to pray that it would not rain; it did not rain in Israel for three and a half years. At the end of that time, God instructed Elijah again to pray for rain, and it rained. God allowed the normal cycle of rain to return to Israel. Wait on God with all patience and perseverance. Help is on the way. Though it may seem late, wait for it; victory is sure as long as the Lord lives—**"for with God nothing will be impossible"** (Luke 1:37). When you pray, pray with understanding, and if you can, pray in the Spirit, get yourself sucked in the oil of His glory, but be wise to step out by faith after you have prayed.

Incoming Calls and Caller ID

Your phone has the ability to identify incoming callers and store the names. Modern-day phones can play all kinds of music (ringtones) and more. People today, especially youth, teenagers, and young adults, are going crazy for wild and hot ringtones. The new phones are able to create video, and today you can even browse the Internet with your phone. Your caller ID helps you to decide whether to respond (answer). Sometimes you really want to take the call, but you have something more important to attend to than unproductive casual talk. Your caller ID is limited as to how many calls it can take or store, which includes incoming calls, outgoing calls, missed calls, and so on.

Your Prayer Line

God also has caller ID. God knows what you are going to ask for in prayer before you even open your mouth. He also knows when we are ready or able to handle that for which we are asking. The good news is God will never tell us what we tell people on the phone, such as, "Can I call you back later, please?" or, "Oh, he is calling again, wasting my time." If the caller has an unknown number or the caller's number is not available, some people ignore the caller. Sometimes people lie, saying, "Let me call you back in a minute." Most of the time, what they call a minute is not a minute; it might be an hour, hours, or days, if they even remember. But our God is not like that. God answers all calls as they come in, all at once. He hears all our hearts' cries and responds to each caller according to His will, purpose, and timing, which is best for us.

God's service area for coverage is unlimited. Millions of people all over the world call on God's prayer line, many at one time. Despite the huge call volume, God receives every call. He responds to every caller. No call is rejected, ignored, or dropped. Thank you, Jesus, is all I am going to say about that! It is a blessing, a great privilege that God hears us and speaks to us. He speaks to me, as little as I am, when no one else wants to hear me or speak to me. Others think I am either foolish or stupid, or that something is wrong with me in my low estate and dark days. There are times when even my dearest friends cannot understand the battle going on within me, the challenges I face. They cannot be of help because all my complaining and explanations don't make sense to them. I am glad that God not only hears me, but also answers my prayers and longs to talk with me. Have you come to a place in your Christian life and walk with God where you are able to receive revelations from God—I mean, to pray and get a word from Him? Have you enjoyed His presence so much that your lips moved, but no words were heard, or have you praised Him with the fruit of your lips so that your hands became instruments of praise and adoration to the God that answers by fire?

Hannah prayed with such great persuasive, powerful, unpopular, selfless passion. Out of the burdens in her heart she cried unto God, until her lips moved, but no sound was heard. She was lost to her world, but was clothed with God's presence. She closed her eyes to the human world and everyday business (distractions) and was alone with God. She approached the throne of grace, just as Queen Esther did before her husband and king, with an irresistible passion, which produced a sweet-smelling savor of her prayers before the God of all possibilities. The high priest Eli misunderstood her hunger, her pain, and her passion for a divine intervention and change in her life as far as childbearing was concerned. The priest Eli thought she was drunk. She was indeed drunk, but not with wine. She was filled with the Spirit, praying through her with groans unuttered.

Hannah Came to God Broken

Hannah was very busy in the spiritual realm taking care of business, a place where flesh and blood cannot prevail, but the power of prayer said with all fervency and simplicity of the heart. She believed that God is and that He is a rewarder of those that diligently seek Him. Hannah came to God broken. She was able to break through in prayer. Today her prayer life is a memorial and a testimony to you and me because she took her stand in prayer. The legacy of her prayer life formed the foundation of the principle of the power of prayer that helped transform her baby boy Samuel into a prophet, a judge, and a priest. This was the very first of its kind in the history of the Israelites' prophetic chronicles. God still speaks. He does reveal things, even the deep things of the Spirit, to those that love Him and put Him above all else.

There are many things [spiritual operations] that you and I will not ordinarily see, which are only unveiled in prayer. God longs to speak with each of us every time we dial the number J-E-S-U-S, but we are not listening. Our hearts are filled with too much junk, which hinders us from being ready to hear from Him or makes us not in the right mind to be able to receive from Him. How many teens, youths, and young adults are going as wild about their prayer lives as they are about their wireless phones? You and I have to sit up and pray for the next generation. When you pray, you can almost tell if your call was a complete call or not, if you allow the Spirit of God to take the lead and not your problems or feelings. When we come before Him, He opens our eyes to see our nakedness (sins), so we can repent and let Him clothe us with His righteousness, which we have in Christ Jesus our Lord.

Too many of us are moved by situations and our physical needs to the place of prayer, rather than being moved by the love we have for God and the zeal to see souls saved and transformed.

Chapter 8

Phone and Prayer Features (Part Two)

Almost every season, new features are added to your phone services. The more features are addictive, the more attached you will become, and the more reliant on the phone you become.

The Internet
Many phones today are able to connect to the World Wide Web (the Internet). You are able to send and receive e-mails, and download whatever you like.

Your Prayer Line
Just as the Internet brings the world into your home, your prayer has the ability to bring heaven down to your world. Heaven came down when Paul and Silas sang and prayed. Heaven will always show up when the people of God call on God in one accord. When was the last time you were able to download stuff from heaven to destroy the strongholds of darkness, those things that try to exalt themselves above the knowledge of God in your life? If you take great delight in the World Wide Web, how about considering heaven's life web? Do you know that most of the good Christian songs you and I enjoy today were

downloaded from heaven's life web? When was the last time you heard from God, the God you call your Father? You hear from people every day. If nobody calls you, you will call him or her so you can talk. As a child of God, how is your communication with your Father and your God? Heaven's life web is what you and I call the Spirit realm.

Hooked by the Internet and Television

I was once caught up in the web of the World Wide Web. I became so engulfed by its power that I did not have time for my spiritual development, my family, and my God. I fell in love with the Internet and television at the detriment of my spiritual life, my family, and my relationship with others. I gave the Internet and television the attention I did not give to my family and my God. How about you—is the Internet, television, games, or your phone robbing you of your time with God or your family? Is the time you spend surfing the Internet, watching TV, or playing computer or video games putting asunder your marriage and your relationship with God? The danger of the Internet, TV, and games is that before you know it, you can spend hours watching, playing games, or browsing the Internet, and you can never have enough of these pleasures. Are you willing to spend that kind of time in prayer and Bible study? It is very sad that some of us can spend hours upon hours on the Internet or watching television, but cannot pray for thirty minutes or an hour without falling asleep. This should not be allowed to continue if you and I must accomplish God's divine purpose and mission for our lives.

The Internet Has It All

The Internet has it all. All the good and bad you can imagine in the world, both past and present, is made available to you and your household through the Internet. It is up to you what you allow into your life and your home through your computer, your television, and your phone. So many things happen on the Internet and on television that if one is not careful and cautious, one will start backsliding without even knowing it until one is drawn away with the world and its desires. God is calling you to come out from among them and be ye separate. Is it wrong to use the Internet, watch TV, use your phone, or play games? Not at all. But when it starts taking from you and your family's time, relationship, intimacy, and fellowship with God, something is wrong. Some bad thorns, evil seeds, can be sown in your spiritual soil (speaking about your spiritual life) without your knowledge because of your carelessness. Pictures, images, and frames will be planted in your mind that may remain for a lifetime. Satan is clever, his deception personified itself in sheep's clothing, and he will set you up and subtly lead you into fantasy, causing you to love to play rather than to pray. You must not underestimate Satan's abilities to distract and oppose you. If God was able to deliver me from the stronghold of the Internet, television, and games, He sure can deliver you, too, if you let Him.

Text Messaging

Your phone is equipped with the ability to store messages, and send and receive text messaging. You are able to write short notes and say all you want with your text messaging for a fee.

Your Prayer Line

I don't know about you, but I do get text messages from the Lord in prayer. Sometimes it's a verse of Scripture that is just enough to comfort my heart and put my mind to rest. There was a time in my life when I was walking on a dark and narrow road, and I was so lost in my agony that I could not pray. When I opened my mouth to pray, tears started flowing down my cheeks. In those dark days, I thought God had abandoned me. I was rejected by men, my biological family and my church family. God comforted my heart by sending me a "text message." A verse of Scripture brought healing to my soul. I knew it was God. Strength came back to me, and my joy was restored. God can text message you anywhere you are at any time, if you are sensitive in the Spirit to hear His whispers of love or still small voice. God's text messages are free. It comes with no restrictions, conditions, or hidden fees at all.

Call Waiting

Your phone is equipped with a device that enables it to alert you, through a beep, of an incoming call while you are on the phone talking to someone else. It is called "call waiting." If you have call waiting as part of your phone service, you will be able to respond to two people by switching between both callers. Nowadays, it is possible to do three-way calling and conferencing, and use your phone as a walkie-talkie.

Your Prayer Line

I have good news for you: God does not have call waiting on His prayer line. He responds to all calls, even if a billion calls come in at once. He has no need for call waiting. Your phone service provider uses customer service agents, who can only talk over the phone sometimes. Sometimes they send you to their stores to be cared for, if there is one in your area. However, God's angels, heaven's customer service agents, are always with us, night and day, just waiting for you to call, twenty-four seven, every week, all year.

Can you say that about your phone service providers, which observe holidays and system upgrade downtimes? Answer for yourself. When talking to some phone service provider representatives, you must be prepared to spend ten minutes or more, sometimes thirty minutes, to get the service you deserve.

Our God operates an "open-door policy"; you can call on Him anytime you want, from anywhere, and anyhow. What can be better than that? This is real freedom. It is life extremely glorious. Do you have the same freedom with your phone service as you have with your prayer line?

Address Book/Contact List

Your phone has an address book that you can use to store important phone numbers. Your phone also has a database (schedule) where you can store your programs or plans, calendar, contact list, to do list, and so on.

Your Prayer Line

From the day you gave your life to Jesus Christ, your admission information was written in the book of life. Only those whose names are written in the Lamb's book will be admitted into the kingdom of heaven. My friend, I hope your name will be found there. God keeps records. He has files on all of us. The file is called "the book of records." In the Old Testament, it was called the book of Chronicles, where the acts of God's chosen men and women and the kings were written. In the New Testament, we have the Acts of the apostles, then the entire Bible from the book of Genesis to the book of Revelation. If God opens your life file, I hope hatred, anger, unforgiveness, and other bad things will not be found in your life's file. The timetable of the whole world is in God's hand, and your times are in His hands, too. So let God take control of your daily life by your committing everything to Him in prayer daily. Please do not forget that our days, nights, the calendar of our lives, and the calculation of our life's span are in the palms of His hands.

Your prayer file: As you keep important numbers on your phone, start writing down your testimonies of God's faithfulness. Your children may need them someday if you are raising them in the way of the Lord, to encourage themselves.

Alarm System

Your phone is equipped with an alarm system. The alarm system will help you to manage your time, if you program it accurately. The problem with any alarm system, though, whether it's your phone or regular alarm, is the battery. If the battery or its power (electricity) goes out, you are in trouble. You will sleep on until God, or something, wakes you up. Perhaps you were a little surprised when I said God will wake you up. It is God who wakes us up every day. Those that He chose not to wake up are those we classify as dead people.

Your Prayer Line

Your prayer line also has an alarm system. When your spiritual life, or light, starts going down, God sends you a warning through people, dreams, and signs, trying to bring you back on track. You and I must be on the alert. We must be very watchful and careful with our spiritual stand and prayer life because the days are evil. Oh, yes, Satan, the devil, knows that his time is short, and he will take every opportunity we give him. The final alarm will not be like your regular alarm system, like the one on your phone or your alarm clock, but a better one. It will be a trumpet, which will be sounded by the angels of God when the Lord Jesus

Christ will show up in the air. Will you be ready when the Lord comes? Will you be there when the roll is called up yonder, or will you be found wanting? May you not be found wanting, in Jesus' name. So get up, wake up, and start putting things right before it is too late.

Prayer life experience: It is better for us as soldiers of Christ to always be ready, prepared and waiting for the Master; our Commander in Chief. Remember the children of Israel in the wilderness, how they often forgot about God when things were better for them and only called on God when things got bad for them. They often forgot that with God, there is no hiding place. He is the only One who knows all of us inside and out, even the things that nobody else knows about. Please learn to pray. Prayer is the essence of our faith in His Word, the anchor of our call, and our service to God on earth. Prayer is our duty, a task that must not be taken for granted. May your prayer battery, your courage, your faith, and your trust in God not go dead. May you not fail God and humanity by neglecting or abandoning the ministry of prayer and the ministry of connecting people to God, in Jesus' name!

Types of Phones

There are different kinds of phones. Numerous styles are being introduced every season—some specially made for young adults, some for teens, some for adults, some for business use, and some for the elderly.

Your Prayer Line

There are different kinds of prayers that you can apply to different situations or circumstances as they present themselves in your life. There are times when you may be too wounded and discouraged to pray. I have been there so many times. The only thing one can do in such a state is give thanks and just be in His presence, rest on His arms, and sleep like a baby. Looking at the life and ministry of Jesus Christ, the prayer of thanksgiving was very dear to His heart. Thanksgiving is one of the many kinds of prayer, which also include the prayer of faith, intercessory prayer, warfare prayer, and so forth. Prayer also has different levels.

The Five Levels of Prayer

1. The praise and worship level of prayer. The praise and worship level of prayer is generally prayed by all Christians who care, who appreciate the goodness of God in their lives.

2. The bread and butter level of prayer. This level of prayer is a general level for new converts who love the Lord and are filled with zeal and passion for the kingdom. It is also a realm when things are going well or you are a little down, but have nothing much to really worry about. I call this level of prayer the give me-give me kind of spiritual teenage level of prayer.

3. The lightweight level of prayer. This level of prayer is attained as one begins to grow in the knowledge of the Lord, from faith to faith. This is a level where the power of prayer is not only talked about, but also lived by faith according to the Word of God. This is a level where you begin to learn to pray by yourself, for yourself, not soliciting prayers. It is also a realm when you begin to have a strong urge that help is needed. This is when things are starting to get out of hand, but are not yet a do-or-die, or life-threatening affair. In this level, you cannot afford not to pray and allow distractions.

4. The "enough is enough" level of prayer. This is a prayer level where your needs are not just wants, but burdens. When divine intervention is really needed with passion, not a shallow kind of prayer, this is the kind of prayer that comes from your innermost being. It is sometimes accompanied by brokenness and hot tears. This is what I call the "Lord, do it now" kind of prayer. This level of prayer often is backed up by fasting. This was the kind of prayer level Hannah operated in first Samuel chapter 1. The church in the book of Acts got to this level, praying for the release of Peter from prison in the Acts of the apostles chapter 12. Jacob, who later became Israel, also operated in this level of prayer when he wrestled with the angel of God until dawn.

5. The "even if" faith level of prayer. Even if God does not do it anytime soon, but you are going to remain steadfast and unmovable in your faith and trust in His faithfulness, you have this level of prayer. This is what I call the stubborn faith level of prayer. Remember Job, how he refused to give up and said, "Though He slain me, yet will I trust Him." Also remember Shadrach, Meshach, and Abednego when they told king Nebuchadnezzar eyeball to eyeball, "Even if our God did not come and save us, we will still not bow to your golden image (man-made god)."

Please note that all five levels of prayer are powerful and competent to overcome the enemy. There are small and big enemies. The first or the later are all adversaries, antagonists, and are ever ready to combat your soul, wellness, and peace. The medication for the common cold may not be strong enough to cure a broken bone. So are the strength and the effectiveness of each level of prayer. All five levels of prayer are based on the kind of mountain, or enemy, that you have to withstand and overcome. You have to apply each level of prayer to the degree of the opposition you are up against, so that the adversary will not have the upper hand in your life. God forbid you end up a prey or victim to the strongholds of the powers of hell, even the power of the darkness of this world.

Another factor that promotes the different levels of prayer is your spiritual maturity and development, based on your personal relationship and connectivity to God. Your obedience to God plays a major role when it comes to the levels of prayer, and you cannot expect the devil to obey you when you are walking in disobedience to God. The closer you are to God, the more you serve Him diligently and trust in Him, the more you will become faithfully connected to Him. Remember, you cannot grow above your prayer life. If you are not powerful in prayer, you will not be powerful spiritually.

Chapter 9

Phone and Prayer Features (Part Three)

People everywhere are falling in love with their phones and the amazing features, as the telecommunications industry seeks ways to improve the comfort of phone use in this digital age.

Going Hands-free

There is a telephone accessory in the market called Bluetooth. Its user is virtually hands-free. You program it, plug it into your ear, and you are ready to go. It is good for handicapped people and those who talk on the phone while driving. Because the phone is hands-free does not mean it is perfectly safe. It is still dangerous to drive and stay on the phone because it distracts you by engaging your mind and impairing your focus and concentration while driving or operating machines.

Your Prayer Line

Your prayer line also is advanced and hands-free. Sometimes you can pray by heart, without even opening your mouth. You can pray anywhere on your own. In ancient times, it was not so; only the priest could go before God in the Holy of Holies to pray for the people. Thank God for Jesus Christ and the price He paid for us on the cross of Calvary. Today we can draw near and are able to come boldly before the Lord of Hosts for ourselves and for our loved ones. The dying man or woman can nod his or her head and God hears his or her prayer (agreement) of salvation. This kind of prayer is totally hands-free and mouth-free. No blood sacrifices anymore; Jesus did it all. Today I can call from anywhere and still be connected to heaven's prayer line. Our prayer line is not limited by weather, nor can the government or anyone on earth limit our prayer line. Lawmakers can oppose or limit audible public praying, but cannot limit the prayer of the heart, the hands-free kind of prayer from our hearts to the heart of God. Today we can worship God all by ourselves as long as we want, anytime and anywhere we want. We are free to enjoy His presence to any degree we want.

Prayer life experience: It is truly amazing, very wonderful, and a great privilege that you and I can relate (pray), or connect, to God individually without any middleman or third party. It is worth celebrating, and this freedom, real freedom, is good, very, very good. Please close this book for a minute and just give thanks to God for loving us so much that He freely gave His only Son, Jesus Christ, for our sins. Thank You, Lord, for bestowing such surpassing love on us. It is truly amazing and very wonderful.

Call Forwarding

Your phone has the ability to forward your calls to another phone, helping you ensure that you do not miss any calls. Your phone transfers your call to the place or phone numbers you have programmed in it. Your phone service provider offers this feature for an extra fee, unless it was originally part of your package deal.

Your Prayer Line

Your prayer line also has the ability to forward messages and calls. The messages that your prayer line forwards is called "revelation." This is how your prayer for confirmation is answered by God. God sometimes does forward messages to our leaders, loved ones, prayer partners, and those who love Him and work according to His purpose through a revelation. The revelations could come as a dream, a word of knowledge, a word of wisdom, a prophetic utterance, a vision, or a still small voice. God uses all of the above to help you make a firm decision, or a confirmation, about what He has already showed you or spoken to you about. God can use anyone and any means He chooses at the time He will forward His messages to us. This is the only difference between your physical phone forwarding and your spiritual phone (prayer line) forwarding. He is God and does things the way He pleases. That is why when you get a confirmation, you will just know that it is God talking to you. The person through whom the confirmation you are expecting from God comes to you may not even have a clue about what is going on, unless you tell him or her about it. Prayers, too, can be forwarded, just as your phone's forwarding feature.

Security Lock/Pass Code

Your phone has a security lock, pass code, or password function installed on it, which prevents unauthorized users from being able to use your phone or access your personal information. If your security lock is turned on, you can set a pass code or password on it. If you forget your pass code or password, you will be locked out of your phone until you are reassigned a temporary password or code, which you can then use to create your new password or code.

Your Prayer Line

Your prayer line also has a pass code in heaven. In the United States, the government uses your Social Security number as your life pass code. God knows all things; He knows every one of us by name, by face, and by blood type. He is our Maker. He has our DNA in His hands, and He cannot forget the work of His hands. All other security can fail, but God will not. God wants you to **"keep your heart with all diligence, for out of it spring the issues of life"** (Proverbs 4:23). He wants you to renew your mind daily by fine-tuning your spiritual focus through the power of His Word. If you refuse to guide your heart by heeding the Word of God, the devil can easily get to your heart, and he can control your whole body and life.

On God's prayer line, you do not have to worry about forgetting your password, but living a life well pleasing to Him. Furthermore, God does not speak to each of us the same way; He speaks to every one of us uniquely, in different ways. With God, there is no identity theft. Nobody can steal your prayer. Satan can only hinder you from waiting on God or make you doubt the faithfulness of God, which could make you lose the harvest of your prayer, but he cannot steal your prayers while they are ascending. It is only with men that we have security needs for passwords or codes to prevent unauthorized access—not with God.

Calculator

Your phone has the ability to function as a calculator. This really makes life easy for many people, calculating simple arithmetic, as the phone is always handy. Today almost every phone has a calculator installed in it.

Your Prayer Line

Our God is a strategic God. Nothing happens in the universe without His knowledge. He adds everything up, and the result of our decision is what we get, good or bad. King David once cried out to God, saying, **"O Lord, teach me to number my days"** (see Psalm 90:12). God did not answer him. If God gave you the sum of your life by telling you how much time you have to live here on earth, you likely would mess up because you would wait until the last minute to put things right with Him. Friend, your days are numbered, and they are adding up. Will you be able to finish what God called you to do on earth before your expiration date (when your time here on earth is terminated)?

No one can truly have a fulfilled life outside Jesus Christ. Natural fulfillment without the spiritual equals no fulfillment because your spiritual fulfillment is the ultimate. It is possible to gain the whole world and lose your own soul. You can *have* God and success, but you cannot *serve* God and success. The time (minutes, hours, days, months, and years) of your life is the sum of your existence, events, activities, hopes, and dreams on earth. There is nothing hidden. Every step you take in life is calculated and recorded. When you calculate your time from now on, include God, prayer, and Bible study in your daily schedule. I pray that the spirit of procrastination will not have dominion over your prayer time, in Jesus' name.

Voice Mail

Your phone has voice mail capability, enabling your callers to leave a message for you if you are absent or busy at the time of the call. You can thereafter retrieve your voice mail messages anytime until you delete them.

Your Prayer Line

I have good news for you. God's prayer line does not have any voice mail because God is able to respond immediately to your call as well as others' calls coming in anytime, any day, and anywhere. Though God responds to every call that does not mean He grants every caller his or her requests according to his or her desires. He is God, and He does things in His own way and timing. If you have any question about that, please call heaven and talk to God. He will be glad to answer all the questions you might have. One thing I can assure you of is God answers prayers; He does not ignore them. **He always makes all things beautiful in His time** (see Ecclesiastes 3:11).

God does not respond to all those who call His prayer line on a first come, first served basis, as your phone service allows. God is well able to respond to all incoming calls at once, without any network breakdowns, twenty-four seven. Anytime you call God, you have access to Him directly, unlike with your phone provider. With it, most of the time, you talk to machines, not people. On God's prayer line, you will never hear, "All circuits are busy; please try your call again later," or, "The network is down at the moment; please call again later." God is obligated to answer your prayers, and He will when your obedience is fulfilled. When your obedience is fulfilled, your prayers can become a stronghold against the strongholds of darkness and bring heaven's power to your world.

Motto Mixer

Your cell phone may have a motto mixer installed in it, although not all phones have this feature. Motto mixers help the phone's user create or fine-tune his ringtones without connection to a computer.

Your Prayer Line

You must be able to mix your prayers with faith to break through in prayer. Here is a list of what you must mix together to have a breakthrough. All the good music you and I listen to from time to time is a mixture of sounds blended together to create a live beat called harmony. There are seven things you can mix your prayer with to create a sweet-smelling aroma of prayer before the throne of God. The seven things to mix your prayer with are:

1. Faith.
2. God's faithfulness.
3. God's faithfulness with love, forgiveness, self-restraint, and your seed (financial giving, time investment, or otherwise).
4. Courage and determination.
5. Burden (deep concern) and expectation.
6. Thanksgiving and praise.
7. All of the above with your obedience to God and His constituted authority in the Lord. Jesus said, "If you love Me, keep My commands" (obey ME!).

Your Phone Privileges

God has impressed it on my heart to write about phone sex and the Internet sex thing. I just have to obey God, and I hope you do not mind. I am not trying to condemn anyone, but humbly bring to you the Word of God as He has impressed it on my heart. God is not happy—He is sad—because of Christians who call Him Lord and engage in phone sex, Internet pornography, and sex games, or whatever you call it. It is true that you have the right and the privilege to use your phone and the Internet and play games as you will. But you need to know that everything you possess and your very self belongs to God. If you have truly and honestly surrendered all to Jesus Christ, let Him have His way in your life. Apart from the physical damages the above things can do to your health and well-being, they weaken your spiritual power and eat up your hunger to seek after God. They drain you of your anointing and pollute your love for God. The same applies to those who call themselves faithful followers of Jesus Christ and still deal or live on all kind of drugs—they want to be high in the flesh and very low in the Spirit.

Stop Operating in the Flesh

My friend, stop operating in the flesh (human knowledge and wisdom). Stand up for God. Stop giving a place to the devil in your life. Your body is the temple of the Holy Ghost, not a temple for drugs, alcohol, or cigarettes. There is a way that seems right to us because we see other people taking that path. That kind of road or path could invariably lead to spiritual death, misery, and anguish. If you are participating in phone sex, sex games, Internet pornography, drugs, alcohol, smoking, or any kind of destructive behavior, the Lord is saying it is time for you to quit. The pleasure of sin is only for a while, but it ends in misery. God wants you to come out from among them and be separated unto Him. Confess your deeds, repent, and do not return to "your vomit." Invite the Holy Spirit to fill up the vacuums those things may have created in your heart and life, in Jesus' name. Another thing concerning phone privileges: Be considerate of others. Do not talk too loud or shout when you are in the midst of others. Respect other people's privacy and dignity; be polite in your approach.

Your Prayer Privileges

As we have phone privileges, we also have prayer privileges. Stop disturbing people by praying too loud. Respect other people's privacy and dignity, especially when you are praying at home and not alone. It is not because those who live with you are devilish or do not want you to pray. If you are not sleeping, please let other people sleep. I believe the best thing to do if you are that person who cannot pray quietly sometimes, like me, is reach an agreement with the members of your household. This is a crucial matter in some homes where Christians and yet-to-be Christians live together under one roof. If people feel you are disturbing them, please train yourself to pray quietly. That is why your alone time with God is called "quiet time." Otherwise, if you really have to pray, go to church and do your loud praying, or pray when you are alone in the house or in the car so no one will be disturbed. Some of us have hindered many people from connecting or coming to God because of the way we take things for granted or are careless sometimes.

Be Wise

You must not fight over where to or where not to pray. The world is big enough for all of us to coexist without any problems. Anyone who is well connected to God can freely enjoy everything that belongs to the Lord and all the works of His hands. He is a God of justice. He is not a partial God, but He is also not a respecter of persons. You must run your Christian race wisely and faithfully so your life will not become an obstacle to anybody trying to come to God. Stop disturbing people with your loud prayers unless you have reached an agreement with people, and they are okay with it, especially when you are praying for their salvation. Saved husbands, wives, fathers, mothers, brothers, and sisters, be wise, stop disturbing your unsaved spouse or child, children [or loved ones] with your loud prayers. If you have tried prayers and are not making a lot of progress toward winning those people for God, try mixing your prayer with love. Let your way of life, your holy conversation, faith, and kindness, win them for God, not your works. Your life is the Bible they want to read. Open unto them the pages of love every day so the Holy Spirit can come in and move upon their hearts. You cannot save or change anyone, nor can you force anyone to be saved or change. It is the Holy Spirit's job to convict, not yours. Your job is to love them and wisely tell them the truth.

I Have Been There Before

I was the first person to be born again in my family and was disowned, cast out, and rejected. The issues that I just told you about, I had to deal them. God told us to overcome evil with good, not by trying to claim our right to pray loud or worship loud in our homes. Love endures all things, and prayer changes things. Pray for those who oppose your love for God or try to stop you from serving God. Love them through it; try to win them with your love. Quarrelling or becoming angry or bitter will not work; it will only make things worse and the sinner more hardened. Jesus Christ did not come to fight in the flesh. Remember, the weapons of our warfare are not carnal, but mighty through God to the pulling down of strongholds. Please develop good prayer manners and "let all things be done decently and in order," according to the Word of God (1 Corinthians 14:40).

Some of us were taught good table manners from childhood. Let us start teaching new converts—babies in Christ—good prayer manners so they do not run into problems in their homes. Let those who are mature help those who are not yet mature to maturity, through brotherly kindness, love, patience, in humility and perseverance and in the beauty of holiness.

Chapter 10

Dangers Associated
With Your Phone

Many people die every year because of cell
phone abuse, driving and talking on the phone at the
same time. Some people operate dangerous machines
and still stay on the phone. Sooner than expected, they
are distracted, and the result of their carelessness is
disastrous. Hundreds of thousands of people get
involved in deadly accidents each year because they
got distracted, lost their concentration, and became
hazardous weapons to destroy their own lives or the
lives of innocent people. Today a lot of industries,
companies, and organizations do not allow the use of
cell phones on the job as long as the employee is on
the clock. Some states in the United States and in some
other parts of the world disapprove of the use of cell
phones while driving, riding in any kind of
transportation, or operating industrial machines. Today
some states make people pay penalties for driving and
conversing on a hand-held phone, and if such people
are involved in any type of accident, fines double. The
phone itself is not bad, but the misuse of it is what is
bad and deadly.

Expressing Anger Through Your Phone

The phone is a means of communication. Some people use it as a tool to express their anger, hatred, and ungodly words that would lead anyone to depression and fear. Nobody is supposed to prey on fellow men, even though people do it out of ignorance and spiritual immaturity. Our weapons of warfare are not carnal (natural). In other words, they are spiritual, meant to fight the devil and his evil hosts who operate through humanity, as a tool to execute his evil deeds. Using your phone to express your anger toward people is a bad thing to do. The person you are venting your anger toward via your phone may be driving and, in the process of listening, may lose control. Do not use your phone to sow discord or depression, or to quarrel. Never tell people words that will make them feel they'd be better off dead or allow devilish words to come from you. So before you get mad and "let loose" on anybody via your phone, please find out what that person is doing first. If that person is driving, ask him or her to call you back, or call that person back.

Prayer Point

Please, pray that you and your loved ones will not become a victim of cell phone abuse. Cell phone abuse, according to research, is a leading cause of devastating automobile accidents today. Let me explain. You only know about yourself. The people driving behind you and ahead of you on the same road you do not know. How would you know if you are driving behind a person who is drunk and confused and trying to get home by any means? If that drunkard decides to stay on the phone while driving in his or her drunkenness, what do you think will happen? Examine the following instances for yourself. I do not know if you are aware of how many innocent lives drunk drivers have taken. The number is painful. Any drunk driver is a road hazard.

Another area to look at is this. You share the road daily with people who use drugs and are very high, driving with one hand, with the other hand holding a hand-held phone in a conversation. What will happen if such a person loses control? This is why you must pray that you and your loved ones will not be a victim of cell phone abuse or get themselves into any other negative circumstance or influence. Yet another area of concern: those who become emotionally charged when they receive bad news, like the death of a loved one. Such emotionally traumatic experiences or conversations can be enough to distract a person and cause an accident if the person receiving the bad news is driving and talking on the phone at the same time. I have seen so many people receive bad news when they were not driving, and they have passed out. You can imagine if such people were on the road.

Your Cell Phone Is Part of You

Believe it or not, your phone number is part of your identity. It can be used to access your personal information. Anybody can impersonate you. Some people will try to impersonate your phone service provider if they can get their hands on your personal information. Some customer service centers today ask for your phone number to access your account, making you and me vulnerable to hackers (information stealers or traders). Just in case you do not know, information is a big money-making business.

Your Phone Versus Your God

I know you value your phone. How well do you value and treasure your spiritual growth and relationship with God? Who has the first place in your life, your God or your phone? If your phone rings while you are praying and fellowshipping with God, whom do you respond to, God or your phone? Who is your closest companion, God or the person calling? With whom or what do you spend most of your time, God, your phone, or the Internet? How much time do you spend in prayer and Bible study, compared to the time you spend using your phone? It is like some people have addictive relationships with their phones. How about prayer or Bible study—are you addicted? You live with your phone and are strongly attached to your phone, instead of living for God.

Your Phone Zeal

People crave phones because of people's hunger to belong and to be connected to friends, loved ones, and family members. As you begin to enjoy the benefits of your phone connection, knowingly or unknowingly, you begin to depend on your phone because your phone and the Internet are easy ways to link to people. Relationships with family, friends, business partners, coworkers, and others revolve around your phone, where you have their numbers stored. You soon become addicted to your phone. When some people wake up in the morning, the first thing they remember is their phone. If they forget their phone somewhere or leave it at home, they will, without fail, return to pick it up. Otherwise, they will be worried about missing calls. To them, life without their phone, games, and the Internet would be boring.

Your Prayer Line

Do you depend on God? Do you maintain a sound and firm relationship with Him, as you do with your phone? How hungry, passionate, and desperate are you for God—as much as you are for your phone? Do you have the kind of intimacy you have developed with your phone, with God? How much time do you spend on the phone with people talking about things that are important or unimportant, necessary or unnecessary? How often do you pray (communicate) with God? How much time do you spend in God's presence and studying your Bible—as much as you remain on your phone? Are you addicted, strongly attached, to God in prayer and to Bible study the same way you are with your phone? How do you feel if you forget your phone at home when you go out, and how do you feel when you forget to pray? How about if you forget to study your Bible one day? With your phone, it is unacceptable for you to procrastinate, but it is acceptable and easy to postpone, put aside, your prayer life and Bible study time for "more pressing needs or responsibilities." How many times do you go to church in a month? How about having a daily quiet time with God? When you talk to people on your phone, you do look for a quiet place to talk freely, don't you, so you will not be interrupted or distracted and will be able to hear your caller or receiver? Is your communication with the men more important to you than your quiet, undistracted communication and fellowship with your God?

Not Happy When Hung Up On

If people hang up their phone on you while you are still talking with them, are you very happy? I suppose not. When you are enjoying a very good conversation on phone with a friend or a loved one, and it cuts off, how do you feel? In fact, when people hang up on you, you feel disrespected, less important, and mad, feeling that the person who hung up on you is mean. When you have important issues to take care of via your phone, do you hurriedly hang up your phone? I suppose not. You relax, taking your time to iron things out!

Your Prayer Line

Why do you hang up your prayer line on God when you call heaven to talk to Him in prayer? If you are not happy when people hang up on you, is God happy when you hang up your prayer line on Him to pick up your phone calls? Your phone call is not a completed call until the person on the other side is able to respond to you and you hear him or her speaking to you or the voice mail. God wants to respond to you if you can stop hanging up (terminating) your prayer line on Him. He is your Father, as you call Him. God wants to communicate with you. God is not a robot, a software device, or an application program you have installed on your phone or computer. He is the living God. He is a person, and He wants you to relate to Him as a person, not as a thing. He is not a product like your phone. God wants to pour His love out on you, if you can stop being in a hurry when you are in His presence in prayer or during worship. Sometimes God has very important things to tell us, but we do not give Him the opportunity to express His love and concerns, and even warn us about evils to come.

God Wants to Enjoy You

God always longs for your presence in His presence, but while He is enjoying your presence in His presence, your phone rings. What do you do most of the time? You turn your back on His face and pick up the call. Sometimes during a church service, prayer meeting, or house fellowship when your phone rings, who takes the preeminence—God or your phone? If it is an emergency call, that is all right; it is understood. Have you ever considered how rude and thoughtless your actions are when you prefer your human caller more than Him? How convicting it is to realize your ill treatment of the God of the universe?

The devil knows that when what the Word of God has for you is about to be brought forth, that is the very time he can prompt someone to call you on your phone. I have personally observed that the majority of the phone calls that come to us during church services come in during the message or prayer time. When you finally go out of the service to answer the call, most of the time, it is either a wrong number or something that is not important, things that could have waited until after the meeting was over. But you have missed the word you came to church to hear or the prayer meeting with God. If you were in the place of God, how would you feel if your child treasured his or her phone more than you? How would you feel if your child were having fellowship with you, and you were enjoying his or her graceful presence, and his or her phone rang, then he or she immediately stops communicating with you, picks up his or her phone, and off he or she goes to respond to the caller, without even saying, "Please excuse me"? As a human being, you would feel offended by the bad and unprecedented behavior of your child. Don't you think God, whom you call your Father, feels the same way? God is a person; He has feelings, just as you do.

Give God Some Respect

You and I most of the time ask people to excuse us when our phone rings before we leave to respond to our phone. Do we respect God the same way when we are in His presence? Is it because we do not see Him face to face that we treat Him any way we like? Every time you hang up your prayer line on God's face to respond to your phone line, the devil gives his demons a high-five and celebrates your lack of respect, reverence for your Maker and God. How would you feel if you were interrupted while in the middle of an important conversation with an important personality like the president of your country? I suppose you would not be happy.

God ought to be the most important personality in your world. He is not happy when you allow your phone call to interrupt your conversation with Him. Please imagine how God feels when you go before Him during your prayer time, just when He is about to open His heart to you, to reveal to you the hidden things of life, and you cut off your prayer line. Do you think God will give Jesus a high-five and say, "This is my beloved son or daughter, in whom I am well-pleased?" The above happens a lot, especially on weekdays, when some of us do "drive-through prayers," just like we do drive-through at fast food restaurants at lunchtime. We are too much in a hurry to wait on God. We find it difficult to obey God's Word, but do not have trouble obeying the children of men, our company, or business policies and procedures. There is not enough time to share with God or in prayer, but we have enough time to spend pursuing the cares, the pleasures, and the glory of this world.

In Men's Presence

If you are in the presence of the president of your country, would you have your phone on? No! It just comes naturally because you have to be respectful and practice good etiquette. When you are conversing with the president of your country on the phone, would you hang up on him because you are in a hurry? I do not think so. What you dare not do in the presence of your human leader or president is what you are taking for granted before the President of all presidents, before the Most High God. Be careful how you play games with your life; that is what you are doing anytime you think you can play games with God.

As we consider the similarities between your phone connection and your prayer connection, you need to be aware of alert messages from the "network provider." Our spiritual line is connected to God. Before your phone connection can be completed, it must connect to the server of your phone service provider for your call to go through in the network and then to the person you are trying to reach. That is why when you get to some remote places, your phone will alert you that there is no network access in the area you are in. This means you will not be able to connect there. If you go to places where you are not supposed to be as a child of God, the Spirit of God also will alert you by prompting you or causing your Spirit not to be at peace. The Spirit of God will alert you that you are out of God's presence and in the enemy's territory. Some of us are too distracted or carried away by the event to be aware of His warnings.

Chapter 11

The Voice of the Children of Men

We are more alert to the voices, signs, and will of the children of men than we are to the voice, signs, and will of God. The sad thing is that some of us feel more comfortable in the presence of men than in the presence of God, or enjoy the presence of men more. If you invite people to party, to eat and socialize and meet new friends, the place will be packed with people. Invite the same people to a prayer meeting, and about 35 percent may honor the invitation. We oftentimes override God's still small voice to please and obey the voices of men. We give place to the devil, the prompting of our flesh, over the prompting of the Spirit of God, especially when we are under stress and are angry. Some places you go require that you turn off your phone or put your phone on silent or on vibration. If the public wants you to respect personal space, or privacy, how about the church of the living God?

Prayer life experience: True prayer is relational—worship and fellowship with God. It should be a glorious time between us and our heavenly Daddy. Never again talk to God as you do to a robot. God longs to communicate with you; let Him respond to you. You must be prepared to come into His presence. Have a relationship first, and then bring your requests. This is not a choice. He knows everything about you and still loves you. The heavenly Father has given you physical life, eternal salvation, and purpose for your life here on earth, and He is preparing a home for you in heaven. (Really, you and I owe it all to Him, in him, by Him, and with Him.) If you have respect for the children of men, what respect do you have for the God of all men? And if you enjoy hearing the voice of the children of men, how about the voice of God, the Father of all Spirits?

No Pay, No Service

If you do not pay for your phone services, your phone service will be suspended or interrupted by your phone service provider, and the provider will continue to charge you even though your service has been suspended or interrupted. If you quit paying for a long time, your provider will turn off your phone.

Your Prayer Line

In your local church, are you faithful in paying your tithes and offerings to God, which go toward the growth and development of your local church? God placed you there to be a pillar of blessing and a vessel of honor for His use. I do know that there are many speculations out there about tithing. I know also that it was instructed by God and must be done if you are a faithful child of God. Your disobedience to God's Word in tithing may suspend or interrupt some of your blessings, just as your phone service provider would interrupt your phone service if you fail to pay for your service. This is why things seem not to be working in our favor financially sometimes. God has said, "Give, and it shall be given back to you." Your input will always determine your output. The measure you give is the same measure that God is going to cause the children of men to give to you. You can never out give God.

Prayer life experience: The law of sowing and reaping is a lifelong principle, which will not change until we get to heaven. "But this I say: He who sows sparingly will also reap sparingly, and he who sows bountifully will also reap bountifully" (2 Corinthians 9:6). Pay your tithe so you do not get into trouble with God. God Himself will place a curse on your finances if you rob Him of His tithe. I do not care what some people tell you about tithing. All I care about is if it is the truth or not, whether it's scriptural. The prayer prayed in disobedience except the prayer of repentance is more or less a waste because it will be corrupted with your disobedience. "Surely the Lord's power is enough to save you. He can hear you when you ask him for help. It is your evil that has separated you from your God. Your sins cause him to turn away from you, so he does not hear you" (Isaiah 59:1-2 NCV).

God's Word Is Truth

As far as God remains true to His Word, His words are settled forever. Paying half or an uncompleted tithe is not acceptable. It turns your tithe into an offering. You still owe God your tithe. The United States' Internal Revenue Service (IRS), for example (or whatever agency or department collects taxes in your country), a man-made department governed by human laws, can take money from you before you even get your paycheck. If you cannot deny the IRS, or other tax agency, their pay, why do you want to deny God His tithe? God's tithe is just one-tenth of your gross income. The people who tell you not to pay your tithe to God are living in disobedience, and they want you to do the same. Can they tell you not to pay your taxes, or question the IRS's or other agency's authority to take your money? If you do not pay taxes, you will go to jail and still have to pay your taxes one way or another, except if it is written off or waived for some reason.

Human Wrath Versus God's Wrath

The people who ask you not to tithe do not fear God; yet, they fear the wrath of the government. Do you want to join with them and partake of their sins and continue in your disobedience? God forbid. God is asking for only 10 percent, in some states in America, for example, people pay 15 percent in taxes. Like it or not, you must pay your taxes. It is the law. In the state of Texas, where I currently live, the government will tell you, if you like yourself, "Do not mess with Texas" because if you mess with Texas, Texas will mess with you. God is saying, "(your name), stop messing with me!" Where do I pay my tithe" a fellow once asked. Your tithe is paid to your local church, not to the television preacher or teacher. That is one of the reasons why you have to belong to a local church.

> "Will a man rob God? Yet you have robbed Me! But you say, 'In what way have we robbed You?' In tithes and offerings. You are cursed with a curse, for you have robbed Me, even this whole nation. Bring all the tithes into my storehouse, that there may be food in <u>My house</u>, and try Me now in this," says the Lord of hosts, "if I will not open for you the windows of heaven and pour out for you such blessing that there will not be room enough to receive it. And I will rebuke the devourer for your sakes, so that he will not destroy the fruit of your ground [business, job or investments], nor

shall the vine fail to bear fruit for you
in the field," says the Lord of hosts.

Malachi 3:8-11

Sometimes your prayer harvests may be delayed because of your disobedience to God's Word. To reopen your phone service line, you have to pay your service provider what you owe. How about your tithe? Ask God for forgiveness, and then pay your tithe. God is the God of mercy. He will let go of the past if you apologize and really want to put things right, so you can start paying your tithe on a clean slate. The choice is yours—either obey God or the people who say do not tithe, people who think they can question God but are not able to question human government's authority to collect taxes. It is up to you; do as you please. It is your life, and you will be responsible for your actions on judgment day.

Payment for Your Phone

When you make payment for your phone service to your phone service provider, do you ask the provider what it does with the money? I do not think so. That is because the representative will ask you if you are planning to rob the provider.

Your Prayer Line

Why do you want to control the affairs of your local church—because you are rich, or because you are privileged to be a blessing to it? I would like to share a personal experience with you. I was invited to preach at a church. After preaching, the pastor invited me to his office for a little refreshment. As I enjoyed myself, I overheard a brother in that church angrily and loudly telling the pastor to give me more money. They had agreed upon a certain amount before the program, but because of the way God moved, this brother thought I deserved more. The humble man of God begged him to be quiet by alerting him that I was in his office and might be listening. He refused and imposed his will on the pastor, and he had to yield to his will. When he gave me the money, I sowed it back to the local church. I told him to call that brother to order, or the church was going to run into a big mess should that kind of behavior continue.

Honestly, I needed that money! It was a good sum. The church would not be blessed and God would not be happy with me if I had taken the money. The brother learned an important lesson when he was told I sowed the money back to the church and that I heard their argument over the money. He became sober and repented. He wrote me a personal letter of apology and sent a copy of his apology letter to his church board and his pastor. He sent me a large check, double the amount they had offered me before. The money came directly from him, not the church. He was humbled and repentant. I got the harvest of my seed. It was an answer to prayer; I mean, the money came right on time. Thank God it all became a win-win blessing. The brother was restored, I was blessed, and their local church was blessed and cleansed. If I had accepted the money because I needed it, what would have happened to that brother, the pastor, and the local church? Think about that!

Respect Your Pastor

So many church people have placed a curse on themselves for trying to take the place of God's Holy Spirit in their pastor's life or local church, either because they are rich or they are busybodies. Even if you are older, more educated, or wealthy, or seem to be more anointed than him or her, please respect the hand of God upon his or her life. If he or she blesses you, you will be blessed, and if he or she curses you, you will be cursed. God honors the cry of His ministers, just as nations respond to the cry of their ambassadors in foreign lands. Your prayer harvest could be hindered or suspended, too, if you disrespect the leadership God has placed over your life. Do not only respect those in authority and treat them nicely and kindly, but do the same to your husband or wife so your prayer harvest may not be suspended or interrupted until you put things right or learn to do things decently and in order.

Prayer life experience: Never despise or disrespect the prayer or the calling of anyone for any reason as long as the person bears the marks of Christ on him or her. You may look at the person's lips and hear his or her words, but God looks into the heart and knows our thoughts. The level of the children of men can never match the level of God. God uses the foolish things of the world to withstand the wisdom of the world. Despise no one, give everyone the opportunity to prove himself, but be careful whom you allow to lay their hands on your head in prayer. If you mess with people, please do not mess with God. Never judge a book by its cover or judge any man or woman of God by his or her financial or educational status. Your success and progress in life may very well depend on the power of that person's prayers when you come in agreement with him or her as the Lord leads you.

Chapter 12

Phone and Prayer Value

Prayer life experience: When you fail to pray or feel you can do without praying, you will no longer have enough power or authority spiritually over your flesh, sin, or any temptation. If you are prayerless, you will run out of the anointing. When your spiritual oil dries up, you will run out of the fire that keeps your prayer life hot, powerful, and dangerous against the kingdom of darkness. In time, you will become spiritually weak because your spirit is at war with your flesh, and you will eventually depart from God's presence.

While in the flesh, your prayer line will be turned into that of complaining or negative confession. The devil is happy when you and I are spiritually cold, prayerless, powerless, and empty. His evil heart rejoices and hopes that you will never pray again. There is joy in hell every day you and I live without praying. Satan is always trying to make friends with the children of God that are prayerful by causing them to live in disobedience. He is happy to see you live in disobedience to God, your parents, and local and spiritual authorities. God will not bless disobedience, nor will He reward unfaithfulness. When you fail to pray, obey God, and be faithful to Him and the authority He has placed over you, you give Satan dominion over you. Satan does not fear you; he is afraid of God's anointing and power in your life.

If you do not live a clean life and possess the anointing of God in your life to withstand Satan, you are in trouble. I hope your case will not be like that of the seven sons of Sceva. (Acts 19:13-19). When the evil spirit cried out, **"Jesus I know, and Paul I know; but who are you?"** (Acts 19:15), they were in prayer, trying to cast out demons, but the demons ended up throwing them out. When your altar of prayer is destroyed, the devil starts winning in your life. When your daily sacrifices of praise and the sweet aroma of your prayer ceases to be offered on the altar of prayer to God, you will fall from the glory of His presence to lust, pride, and worldliness, and your hunger and passion for the Lord will start dying gradually and quietly. Repair your altar of prayer today like Elijah did, and then call down the fire of God to consume anything and everything that easily hinders you from praying in Jesus' name. It is only when the power of God falls upon you that you will know that the Lord is God who loves and also the consuming fire that purifies our motives and actions.

You and Your Phone

So many Christians today travel or go on vacation without their Bibles. A pastor friend once told me, "My vacation is my vacation. I am just going to enjoy myself. No Bibles, and no prayer meetings, nor will I take any calls from my church people, and I am going to have fun." I told him, "It is not wrong for you to have a vacation; we all need to refresh ourselves from time to time so we can keep on strong. But what if God went on vacation?" He was shocked. "Are you a soldier of Christ?" I asked. He said, "Yes!" I responded, "Your vacation should never make you any less of a warrior for God. The devil does not take vacation. He knows his time is short and is busy working overtime, trying hard to bring you down. Taking a vacation is not bad, and I am not asking you not to take a vacation. All I am saying is that it must be done to please God or move you toward God. If it is not going to make you more prepared as a soldier of Christ, knowing that the days are evil, do not take a vacation. As a soldier of Christ, you must always be on alert and sensitive to the Spirit of God, our Commander. No matter how soldiers have fun, they are always ready for duty if they are called upon."

Learn From King David

King David took a vacation while his army was at war. The children of Israel are still suffering from the sin of King David's carelessness during his vacation while his men were at war. Rest is good, but you must be on guard twenty-four seven. Some Christians, even ministers of God, go on vacation without their Bibles, but do no travel without their phones. In fact, the phone is the very first thing that comes to mind as they prepare for the journey. The phone is fast becoming a personal companion to so many people. A brother once said to me, "It is like living in the dark if you do not have a phone." My question to him was, "Were you living in the dark before the cell phone came into existence?" His answer was, "Well, this is the new age, but that was in the olden days."

On Vacation With Your Phone

I was privileged to travel with a Christian brother not too long ago. During the flight, I asked him to bring out his Bible so I could share with him the revelation God had just given me that day. My friend responded by saying, "I am not going to Dallas to preach; I am on vacation. Why should I travel with my

Bible, by the way?" It was very sad the way he responded to me, as if it were a natural thing for a minister to travel without his Bible.

Where Is Your Phone?

"Where is your phone?" I asked. He handed his phone to me in the twinkling of an eye. He did not know where I was going with my question. He started telling me about the kind of plan and features offered by his service provider. He told me about the features he had on his phone and that he can call nationwide and so forth. Then I asked him, "Which of the two is more important to you as a soldier of Christ—your Bible (the sword of the Spirit), or your phone?" He became quiet. I proceeded to ask, "Which of the two do you treasure more—your Bible, or your phone?" He was still quiet. Finally, I told him, "Your phone helps you to relate with men, and all you hear are the voices of the children of men. The Bible develops your relationship with God. The Bible is the Word of God, the food your spirit feeds on, and the sword of the Spirit. I have not physically seen God, but have seen Him and heard from Him daily through His Word, the Bible." He broke down in tears and said, "I am so sorry. I have never thought of it this way. God, please forgive me." Further, I asked him, "How can we have a revival when we do not spend time in the presence of the Lord? We want to abide under the shadow of the Almighty, but we do not want to dwell in His secret place. The Bible is our life manual." He was broken and promised to make a change, to make his Bible his companion, not his phone or iPod.

Prayer life experience: There must be a connection between your faith and your prayer before you pray. There must be a connection between your hope and your belief after you prayed, and your expectation for the physical manifestation of your prayer harvest. Your faith must be tied to your hope; you must not leave any room for unbelief. Most prayers fail because we tie our faith to how we want it done. As children of God, you and I must come to a point in our Christian race where self and complaining must give way so we can truly and confidently seek the face of God, not the faces of men. We must come to a point where nothing else matters but God, His faithfulness, and His unsurpassed love, and we know that it is all about Him and not about us.

Sleeping With Your Phone

Many of us sleep daily with our phones by our bedsides, while the Bible is kept on the living room bookshelf, where the devil likes for it to be, untouched and unread, until another church service. For example, my wife and I visited our Christian neighbors, who at the time were going through challenges. The Lord placed it on our hearts to go and encourage them and remind them of His love and faithfulness in times of trouble. While we were there, the Lord gave me a Scripture to share with them. I told the couple and their son to get a Bible. I said I would like us to read it together before I explained what God ministered to me. After ten minutes of silently waiting, the man of the house turned to his wife, and the wife turned to her son and asked, "Where is the Bible?"

Missing Bible

Then they all went into their rooms, and none of them came out with a Bible. "Where is the Bible?" they continued to ask one another. Then their son said to his mom, "I think the Bible might be in the trunk of the car. Mom," he said, "Remember, you asked me to keep it in the trunk of the car last Sunday." She said, "Yes, that is true. Please go and get it." We came to visit with them on a Saturday evening, which means the Bible had been in the car trunk for seven days! The little boy ran out to go get the Bible from the car trunk. Immediately after the boy left, the phone rang. It was the cell phone of the man of the house. He responded to the caller immediately and said, "Pastor, just a minute." He stood up and left our presence. His son brought in the Bible from the car while the man was still on the phone. His wife went in and reminded him that the pastor and his wife were waiting for him. We heard him in the hallway saying, "Can I please call you back in about ten minutes or so? Okay, bye." When he sat down, he said, "Sorry, pastor. That was a friend of mine. I will call him back when we finish." When they settled down, we informed them that God sent us to encourage them to be firm and to keep trusting in His faithfulness, but they must give the Word of God a valuable place in their lives. The fact that the Bible was in the car trunk from Sunday until we visited with them that Saturday evening meant there had been no Bible reading or study in their family.

Three Weeks Later
The man saw me, three weeks later, about to park my car one evening, and he ran to me praising God. He told me how God has given them victory. He also said, "Thank you for your boldness to rebuke us about not reading our Bible and leaving it in the car. That night after you all left, we had our first home Bible study as a family. We were so blessed by it. Our son was thinking about joining a cult in his school. My wife read a portion of the Bible that divinely addressed it that day, and my son opened up. He said he thought that joining a cult was the same thing as joining a church. His friends in school had told him that God is the Lord of the occult and everything in the world. We should rejoice in the truth, celebrate the truth. Jesus Christ is the truth. "Jesus said to him, **'I am the way,**

the truth, and the life' " (John 14:6a, emphasis added).

Prayer life experience: It is foolishness and immaturity that make people envious, jealous, and sad toward the people they prayed for when God begins to prosper and bless them more than themselves. This is a fallen state and an attempt to join forces with Satan to destroy. Let this never be said of you. Be a blessing, not a curse; a builder, not a destroyer. Start building bridges, not walls. Instead, rejoice when your brother or sister in the Lord is blessed, and God will bless you, too, by so doing.

Spending a Lot of Money on Phones

I noticed that a lot of people spend a great deal of money buying new phones and beautiful handsets or headsets. They spend a lot of money upgrading phone accessories and their features. Tell me how many Christians spend even thirty dollars a month to buy Christian books or CDs to enrich their spiritual lives and development? How many Christians have bought themselves new Bibles in the last five years? Instead, some people are still using their old, torn Bibles that their grandpa or ma bought for them a long time ago. You spend so much money upgrading your phone and its features. How much do you spend on missions, on helping a brother, a sister, a neighbor, or a local church in need? Think on these things, and redirect your spending. I am not saying do not spend on yourself, but consider others who are in need, too. Do not be selfish. Learn to give, for it is more blessed to give than to receive.

Not Investing in Bibles

Today a lot of Christians are expecting to receive free Bibles. If they do not get a free one, they just keep using their old, torn Bible, even to the extent that some of the pages are missing. I often see people come to church with very expensive cell phones, but their Bible covers have long torn apart, and they cannot find their Bible's back cover anymore. Some people use tape or rubber bands to try to put their Bibles together, so they will not have to buy new ones. Also, a lot of us procrastinate when it comes to studying our Bibles. Do you do your best to feed your spirit man (the Spirit of God in you) as you feed your earthly man (your body)? You read your Bible only when you go to church or only on Sundays. Feed your spirit man at least once a day. You feed your physical body three times a day, but starve your spirit of the bread of life if you do not study the Word of God. Your earthly body came from dust, and to dust it will return someday, but your spirit will return to God. You care about your phone and your relation to the children of men your whole life, while not taking care of you, the real you, your soul, the only life you have.

Balancing Our Lives

As Christians, we have to be able to balance our spiritual lives with our physical lives. Things can begin to go wrong with your stand and relationship with God from the moment you begin to compromise your spiritual stand with your fleshly motivations, standards, and desires. When you give your natural life here on earth the preeminence over your spiritual life, your flesh (body) will begin to dictate your pace in life. The flesh loves to be in charge, and if you allow it, it will control your spiritual hunger and zeal for the Lord. When that happens, please know that backsliding has started. The first sign is falling asleep or letting your thoughts drift to other things during prayer or Bible study. Secondly, when it is church time, you lose the passion, hunger, and joy to go. Thirdly, when you manage to get to church, you become personal about the message or sermon. If you are experiencing any of the above, you need a personal revival before things get out of hand. Go and seek help and cry out to God in prayer before it is too late.

Charging Your Phone

How many Christians today watch over their spiritual or prayer lives like they do their phones? How many Christians are as consumed with the zeal of the Lord as they are with the things that do not make a spiritual impact on the lives of men? How many are as passionately on fire for God to reach out to unbelievers as they are for non-spiritual things? Not enough! How many Christians today wake up and go out every day without spending time in the presence of God or return at night and go to bed without even praying? A whole lot! How many Christians today forget to charge their cell phones or make it ready for use the next day? Very few! After working, picking up your children from school, and going home very tired, you do not forget to charge your phone before going to bed. Rarely do you forget! But how about praying—do you forget to pray before going to bed? Often! When will you pray, when you get to church on Sunday? When will you read the Bible? Will that be on Sunday when you get to church? "God will understand" is always the answer. That is bad business.

Taking God for a Fool?

Sometimes we take God for a fool. If your phone provider does not accept your reasons for not paying your bill, and you know that your phone would not work if uncharged, what makes you think God will understand your negligence to the call of duty? You are a soldier on active duty if you are an active Christian. You are too tired to pray when you are not too tired to charge your phone. Have you forgotten that you are a soldier at war? Why should you sleep without fortifying yourself by praying? Would you want to sleep unarmed, uncovered, and unsecured and want to face the enemy with your bare hands? If Satan and his evil hosts are going about their business like roaring lions seeking whom they may devour, what will happen if they find you sleeping not fortified (not covered by the blood and prayer) or playing when you are supposed to be in the secret place of the Most High (the place of prayer). Tell me why you will not wake up the next day to be greeted with disappointments or troubles sown in the soil of your life while you were sleeping on duty and playing instead of praying?

Chapter 13

The Parable of Jesus

Another parable He put forth to them, saying: "The kingdom of heaven [your Christian life] **is like a man who sowed good seed in his field; but while men slept** [you forgot to pray, but you did not forget to charge your phone], **his enemy** [the devil] **came and sowed tares** [bad seeds—problems] **among the wheat** [the blessings] **and went his way. But when the grain had sprouted and produced a crop, then the tares** [the bad seeds the enemy planted while you were sleeping not fortified] **also appeared. So the servants of the owner came and said to him, 'Sir, did you not sow good seed in your field? How then does it have tares** [bad seeds]?' **He said to them, 'An enemy has done this.' The servants said to him, 'Do you want us then to go and gather them up?' But he said, 'No, lest while you gather up the tares you also uproot the wheat with them. Let both grow together until the harvest.' "**

Matthew 13:24-30a

Who knows if our careless decisions and prayerlessness are responsible for the many tares, or problems, you and I may be growing along with in our lives or relationships today? The master said to them, Leave the tares alone, but think about it—what do the tares in the above parable represent in your life?

Prayer life experience: Pray and ask God to remove any seed that He has not planted in your life, and the seeds you have allowed to be sown in the soil of your life through your bad decisions, in Jesus' name. Pray and uproot every satanic implant in your life, home, and family, in Jesus' name. For the tree that cannot be uprooted, like your wife or child, parents, and in-laws, pray that the Lord will give you the grace to carry that kind of cross and the wisdom you need to be as harmless as a dove among wolves, and that He may deliver you from household enemies.

Do Not Let God Make You Pray

May God not make you pray by allowing evil to knock on your door to wake you up or get you prepared for the fight of your life. So be wise, get up, and do all you possibly can to pray. Do not let God make you pray! That's why you must WATCH AND PRAY.

"Watch and pray, lest you enter into temptation. **The spirit indeed is willing, but the flesh is weak**" (Matthew 26:41, emphasis added).

Do not wait to start praying at the hour of temptation; it may be too late then. We ought always to pray and not to faint according to our Commander in Chief and prayer leader, Jesus Christ.

Prayer life experience: If you are prayerful only when things are bad and difficult, you are not a good friend to God. A good friend stays closer than a brother. The effectual relationship of a good friend is not controlled by circumstance, but by love. God needs your fellowship; He longs to see you daily in His presence. He is still seeking true worshipers, who will worship Him in Spirit and in truth. Stop seeking His hands and blessings instead of His face. Learn to love God for who He really His, His person, not His goodies. Do not let circumstances determine your relationship with God, but love God with all your heart, power, and might in season and out of season.

Falling Asleep While Praying

Do your best not to fall asleep while you are praying; it is extremely dangerous. You do not want to sleep on the battlefield, especially now that the devil is doing all he can to perfect his evil deeds because his time is short. If you hardly sleep while talking on the phone, why should you sleep during prayer time? You enjoy talking on the phone, smiling, and laughing, even though the person on the other end of the phone may not see you. Why not enjoy the presence of God the way you enjoy your communication on the phone with men?

Prayer life experience: If you are too tired to pray, just give God thanks. Apply the power of the shed blood (cover your life, home, family, and spiritual walls with the power of the Lamb's blood) and sleep. You will be a foolish soldier if you are not ready. The enemy will not take you for granted if he finds any grounds or opportunity to attack you. Moreover, it is a bad habit for you to be sleeping in the battlefield all covered up beneath your comforter. You are too precious to God and the body of Christ to live your life carelessly. When you fail to pray, you are setting yourself up for a satanic attack. The truth is you are tempting the devil to dare you. God's grace does not cover foolishness; it covers only mistakes.

Give No Place to Fear

When the enemy threatens you through the children of men or by circumstances, do not rely on man for help, and do not become fearful. God has not given you the spirit of fear, but of power and sound mind. During hard and trying times, do your best not to live in fear or allow it to control your prayer mood. The prayer you said mixed with fear will not be sweet smelling to God. Such a fearful prayer is just like the offerings offered with grudges and complaining. Please understand that sometimes our sins and our flesh pollute the things we present to God. God commands us to pray by faith, not by fear. In fact, fear will cripple your faith in God because it is the opposite of faith; it is the stronghold of doubt and unbelief. If Daniel was fearful, he would have been eaten up by the lions when he was thrown into the lions' den. His boldness was developed prior to his lions' den experience in prayer, and this prepared him for the day of battle.

Prayer life experience: Do not rejoice because your prayer can move mountains; rejoice because you have a God who answers prayer and can move any mountain. For without God, we can do nothing! Let your prayer begin with faith, process by faith, and release by faith. Never take the glory for answered prayers or say it was because you prayed. Your prayer was answered because God chose to do so. God will not share His glory with anyone. Remember, He is the Author and the Finisher of our faith. And you must not take credit for any prayer you said. Do not ever ascribe praises to your faith. Give God all the glory for all answered prayers, for in Him we live, move, and have our being. Give no place to the devil for any reason. **"Be anxious for nothing, but in everything by prayer and supplication, with thanksgiving, let your requests be made known to God"** (Philippians 4:6).

Your Family and God's Call on Your Life

Do you wish for your family and friends to learn how to appreciate the call of God upon your life and prayerfully support you? Do you want them to help you accomplish the call of God on your life instead of allowing you to fall victim to circumstances and personalities you come in contact with on your life's journey? You are uniquely made and created by God to fit into the purpose for which He has called you. All you need from loved ones is their prayers, encouragement, edification, and 100 percent support.

Dear Family and Friends

If you cannot pray for those God has called out for His use, do not talk about them. If you cannot encourage them, do not frustrate them. If you cannot support them, do not deceive them with your vain promises. If you are not going to stand in the gap for them, do not set them up or sell them to their enemies. If you are willing to uplift them, do not bring them down. If you cannot help them to become well connected to God, they do not need your connection. If you cannot help them become the person God wants them to be in Him and for Him, they do not need you in their lives. Please do not call them your friends, brothers, or sisters if you are not going to help them get to the arena of success.

Greatly Needed by Everyone

The kind of friend you need is that person who will be your strength when you are weak. You need a friend who will not stab you from behind while smiling with you at the same time. You need a friend who will not allow the enemy to use him or her against you or will not help make room for the enemy to come in and attack you. You need a friend who can correct you when you are wrong, rebuke you as necessary in love, not a judge or condemner. You need a friend who will be a blessing to you, a godly example, not a hindrance or a stumbling block to your life, call, and ministry. If anybody calls you a friend, let everything he or she does, all that person's dealings and interactions with you, move you toward God, not toward men. There are too many battles to fight and enough distractions already from the opposition; you do not need any more entanglement with those who claim to be godly but do not act godly.

This includes those who pray or speak in tongues, talk like holy angels, but do not speak the truth. It also includes those who claim to have great faith in God but are not faithful to Him, who call Him Lord with their lips, but their hearts are far from Him. As for me, Joseph Blessing Omosigho, I need a friend with whom to make heaven, so that when we both meet in heaven, I can say to him or her, **"Well done, my good and faithful friend. Welcome to life, power, and glory."** My friends, relatives, church leaders, and members of the body of Christ, if you don't give me anything else all your life, that is okay with me, but please give me your love and prayers from a sincere heart. If you can honestly do that for me with all your heart, I will be forever grateful, and you would have helped me a great deal. All I long for is to be the person God wants me to be for His glory. We must truly love one another to the end. Jesus did. He gave His life for us because He truly loved us. We ought to do likewise to one another as children of Love. God is Love.

Chapter 14

The Power of Prayer

The power of prayer is too great to be underestimated by anyone who truly loves the Lord and wants to see the kingdom of this world become the kingdom of our God. Satan cannot stand any prayer offered from a clean heart. I mean the prayers that are Bible-based, flavored with humility and thanksgiving, and rendered to God with faith. Satan knows those who know their God. The power of your prayers is determined by the acts of your obedience to God. To obey is always better than sacrificing. The anointing of the Spirit comes in, with the power of prayer. The power of prayer is the power for warfare. When you come into His presence, in prayer, it is good to mix God's Word with your faith in obedience. Psalm 5:2 says, "Give heed to the voice of my cry, my King and my God, for to You I will pray."

Prayer life experience: The devil hates to see you live totally for God or live a life well pleasing to Him. He enjoys it if you live in disobedience, playing instead of praying.

Prayer Is a Privilege

Nothing in this world is greater than the grace you and I enjoy in Christ. Nothing in this world is worth giving up eternal life for. It is a huge privilege that we are able to pray and relate to God, our King and Maker. Tears always fill my eyes every time I think of God's unfailing love, how He loved me enough to die for me while I was yet a sinner. When I look at all that Jesus Christ did and has continued to do for me, I am amazed. If I had all the money, knowledge, and power, I would not have been able to save myself. I would have been lost forever if not for the sacrifice, the price Jesus paid for me on the cross of Calvary! It is extraordinarily amazing that someone like me can call God my Father. Serving God is a privilege, and the ability to pray is also a privilege, not a right. We are saved by grace, not by works. It is the Spirit of God, not us, that causes and helps us to pray.

The Heart That Prays

A prayerless heart will end up becoming a heart filled with complaints, but a prayerful heart will be filled with the joy of the Lord. There is power in your mouth. It is your mouth that expresses what you have in your heart. You are the one who determines how you use your mouth, whether to complain and murmur or to pray and praise God. God does not listen to complaints; He listens to prayers. So quit complaining and start praying. God still answers prayers, just as He did in the book of the Acts of the apostles and at other times in the past.

Through prayer, the lives of many have been changed and transformed for God. Nations and kingdoms have been changed and blessed. Men, women, and children have obtained the promises of God. The mouths of lions and other animals have been shut. Chronic sickness and diseases have been healed by the power of God through the ministry of prayer. Through the ministry of prayer, the weak are made strong, and women and men have received their dead children and spouses back to life by faith. The chains of limitation and imprisonment have been broken, and prisoners have obtained freedom. People everywhere have obtained great deliverances through the power of prayer. The power and the glory of prayer are seen everywhere people know the value of prayer. The footprint of prayer is clearly seen all through the pages of the holy Scripture. Some mountains (limitations) will not move until you pray. If you want anything to move, you speak to it; nothing moves until you speak. **"For verily I say unto you, That whosoever shall say unto this mountain, Be thou removed, and be thou cast into the sea; and shall not doubt in his heart, but shall believe that those things which he saith shall come to pass; he shall have whatsoever he saith"** (Mark 11:23 KJV).

Prayer life experience: Life and death lie in the power of your mouth. When you pray, you bring forth the life and the light of God to shine on your path. On the other hand, if you fail to pray, you will not be able to withstand the stronghold of death, which represents destruction, failure, and disappointments.

We Must Embrace Prayer

I strongly believe that the church of God is going to experience a great revival very soon. God wants to pour down His power upon us as He promised to do in the last days, but there is a problem, a hindrance, and a limitation. God will not pour out His power or the fullness of His Spirit on a weak church. Why? This is because the revival will not last if God pours out His Spirit on the church, the body of Christ, while we are weak, striving, and in disagreement with one another. The majority of our churches' members are not driven by God, but by money. They are people-centered, not Christ-centered. We enjoy visiting with one another, spending time with and talking long hours on the phone with one another, being on the Internet, or playing games. But when it comes to prayer, we take the grace of God for granted. Search the Scriptures, and you will see, when the people of God prayed, the power of God came down. The Spirit of God was poured out in Acts chapter 2 when the people of God gave themselves to the ministry of prayer. We will experience revival when the fear of God increases in us and the fear of men and Satan decreases. We will be impacted, **"praying always with all prayer and supplication in the Spirit, being watchful to this end with all perseverance and supplication for all the saints"** (Ephesians 6:18).

Satan Is Prepared

The devil is not ignorant of our quest or hunger for more of God, but some of us are ignorant of his evil scheme and devices. The battle line has been drawn, and the devil is fully prepared to pour out his evil power on his agents and ministers to operate in the fullness of his wickedness. We are not ready. We are busy browsing the Internet, playing games, fighting with one another, and gossiping. If we do not sit up and take our stand, we might be taken unaware. The devil is trying very hard to keep you and me away from prayer. He occupies our days with socialization with the children of men and causes us to become complacent and indifferent with God.

Sometimes the first thing people think about when they wake up in the morning is their phone, which sets the pace for the rest of their day. You want to talk on the phone during every bit of spare time you have. You start your day talking on the phone and end your day talking on the phone. I am not saying you should not socialize or talk to people; I am simply saying that there is time for everything. Learn from Daniel; he was a man of prayer. Prayer was his passion, and nothing on earth could stop him from having His quiet time with God. He enjoyed praying and loved to tarry in the secret place of the Most High. No wonder he found a place to hide during his time of temptation and persecution. "Now when Daniel knew that the writing was signed, he went home. And in his upper room, with his windows open toward Jerusalem, he knelt down on his knees three times that day, and **prayed** and **gave thanks** before his God, **as was his custom since early days**" (Daniel 6:10, emphasis added).

The freedom you and I enjoy in Christ today was attained by prayer. Jesus started His ministry by prayer, and He ended with prayer. How do you start and end your day? Is prayer a priority to you? If Satan will not quit fighting, working very hard to steal, kill, and destroy, should you and I quit fighting or praying? I suppose not. We will not be able to overcome the devil by mere conversing on the phone; we will get our victory on our knees.

Prayer life experience: If Satan cannot succeed in helping you yield to temptation and sin, he will send distractions to draw your attention from God and prayer. Remember, Eve was distracted, and she fell. Abraham was distracted and slept with his servant because of the obsession of his own wife, Sarah. Is your phone, television, Internet, computer, or games distracting you from praying? Watch out! Stop taking God's grace for granted. **"Continue earnestly in prayer, being vigilant in it with thanksgiving"** (Colossians 4:2).

Your Connection With Man

You should never be more connected to people than you are to God. It is time for you to clothe yourselves with the garment of prayer, not with the praises of men. If you truly long to see the demonstration of the power of God in this world today and in your life, you must be prayerful. Honestly speaking, some people will not believe until they see the manifestation of the power of God in action. If we need revival, we must pray without ceasing. If you want to remain neither cold nor hot, you may be left behind in the forthcoming move of the Spirit of God. I hope you will not draw back on the day of battle or become prey to the devil you have been praying against.

Staying on the phone or the Internet for many hours or playing games will not bring down the gates of hell as the power of prayer would do. If you want to overcome the way Jesus did, then do as He did; give yourself to the ministry of prayer. Jesus was a man of prayer. I am not against friendship, but God is asking for you to come back home, to the place where you first met Him. Return to your first love, when God was all you knew and all you wanted to know, before you started backsliding. Why not do so now?

Your phone, the Internet, and games were invented by men, and they are useful only here on earth. Prayer was begot by God through faith and was made perfect by the blood of the Lamb on the cross of Calvary. When the children of men were not able to move toward God through legalism, church politics, theology, Judaism, and religion, God came down to earth to move man unto Himself.

Through Your Phone

Through your phone as you have conversations with the children of men, you will gain tremendous insights into and become familiar with the world and its operations. The world's systems give you a promissory note of pleasures and fun, which you will enjoy but for a while. Comparatively, through prayer, you will gain tremendous insights into the spirit realm and become familiar with the operations of both good and evil spirits. You also will experience the everlasting joy that flows from the very throne of God, which will fill your inner man with living waters.

Prayer life experience: The streets of gold are not prepared for people who in their lifetime did all they could do, to please the children of men or themselves. They are for those who have given all in order to gain Christ. They are for those who daily carry their cross, following our Lord and Savior Jesus Christ, our chief Shepherd, as He leads the way, and those who live a life of holiness, who serve God in spirit and in truth. They are for those who dare to make a difference and spend tremendous time in prayer travailing for the souls of sinners to be saved and for the saved not to be lost.

Jesus Prayed

You and I know very well that Jesus Christ is Lord and that He is God (John 1:1). Jesus Christ had to pray while on earth to survive, overcome, and bring down the power of God to our world. Why on earth should you and I take prayer for granted? Was it not the power of prayer that transformed the destiny of Jabez? Jesus Christ is not relaxing in heaven; He is busy praying for you and me day and night, making intercession for us so that the devil will not destroy us. Jesus is praying for us so that the devil and his evil hosts will not have the upper hand in our lives and families. We lost our focus on eternity because of distractions, because we are oftentimes too busy pursuing the cares of this world and pleasures of life that we forget that the ultimate reason we exist is to love God and then our neighbors.

The apostles, the disciples of Jesus Christ, were able to accomplish mighty works in the book of Acts of the apostles because they gave themselves to the ministry of prayer until they were endowed with the power from on high. Great men and women, God's generals in time past, all devoted their lives to the ministry of prayer and were greatly used of God to reach the nations for Christ. The Azusa Street Revival we celebrate in America today was birthed by the power of prayer. If we want to see the hand of God move like never before on earth, we must devote ourselves to the ministry of prayer. Prayer should not be a casual exercise or a thing to do when we feel like it. Prayer should not be reserved only for the day of trouble. Jesus Christ, our example, made it clear, "We all ought always to pray and not to faint." The time is coming, and now is when we will not just say prayers, but live a life of prayer and be filled with the fullness of God's power until the day of glory.

The Machinery of the Church

Prayer is the machinery that moves the church, just like a ship has machinery and a mechanism that moves it. The ship is big, and so is the church. The steering and control of the whole ship lies in a little handle. The ship is powered by the handle's movement; with the handle, the captain of the ship is able to maneuver the ship as he will. How about the thing that steers and controls the movement of the church? you might ask. The whole church, the body of Christ in her entirety, is controlled by a tangible part of your body called your tongue; for therein lies the life and death of the church. Oh, yes, the rise and fall of many lie within the process of your mind joining forces with your heart and the power of your tongue. The words from your mouth are honored by God or treasured by Satan based on their proceeds.

Heaven awaits your prayer to set things in motion on the earth, working toward making all things work together for the good of humankind. The devil also awaits your negative confession to deploy the powers of hell into active duty, working day and night, twenty-four seven, to bring your negative confessions to pass. The time has come for the church of God to put aside the things that easily beset us, the things of flesh—denominational barriers and all the man-made traditions, ways, styles, and types of worship systems and schemes that will not save the souls of men or connect humanity to God. **"But the end of all things is at hand; therefore be serious and watchful in your prayers"** (1 Peter 4:7).

United in Prayer

With all due respect and memorial, we must stop trying to please our denominational founding fathers' beliefs and traditions. It is time for us to turn from the ways of men to the ways of God. The power of unity is the power that propels the wheels that control the power of prayer. We must make Jesus Christ our goal. We must give His Word total preeminence above all else and make His mission our passion. Put aside the traditions of men and their various ways, styles, rules, and manners of worship. If we must prevail against the gates of hell, it's time to arise and tell the devil, "Enough is enough!"

Our Agreement Is Our Power

We all pray at our local churches, but we are not making a substantial impact in our nations because we are divided and do not agree. **"Can two work [walk] together, unless they are agreed?"** (Amos 3:3).

If our prayer effort is not blessed, we will not be blessed until we come before God in agreement. Will you be able to drive your automobile without the machinery that holds its engine together? I suppose not. So why do we want to move the church forward and upward without the machinery of unity and prayer? For your automobile to work perfectly for you, all its machinery and mechanisms have to work together in agreement. Why can't you and I, children of one God, come together as one to move the church of God forward by our prayers? To be honest with you, my friend, I believe we can do it. We must put all our differences aside and focus on the bigger picture, so we can jointly reach the world for Jesus Christ and see Him glorified on the earth.

Chapter 15

You, Your Phone and Prayer

God will not anoint anyone He cannot count on, nor can He commit the treasures of heaven into the care of anyone who is not a good steward. You cannot lead God's people if God cannot lead you, nor can God trust you with His power if you cannot trust Him enough to obey Him. Your phone connection links you with the public and helps you abide with men, bearing earthly fruits because that which is of the flesh will produce after its kind. Your prayer connection links you with God and helps you abide in Christ, for without Him you can do nothing, bearing spiritual fruits because that which is born of the Spirit is Spirit.

Your phone connection shapes you into the likeness of men, but your prayer connection shapes you into the likeness of God. Talking too much to men may get you into trouble sometimes. Talking too much to God will save you from a lot of trouble. Prayers create peace around your life and subdue your craving for the lusts of the world and the pride of life. It is possible to conquer the world and not be able to conquer your thoughts and the love of the world. That is why you and I must embrace the power of prayer, because prayer can, without a doubt, help you overcome a lot of temptations. Let us learn from the life and ministry of the one-time strongest man in the world.

Samson: a Man of Like Passion

Samson was a very powerful and strong man in the flesh, anointed and empowered by the Spirit of God to do the unusual. It is true, he was anointed by God, and God gave him supernatural strength, but he was not a prayerful man. He knew the power and the glory of prayer, but chose to ignore it. This man prayed desperately for water, and it sprang forth from the jawbone of an ass. One can conclude that he only prayed when he was in trouble or when he desperately needed divine intervention, just like some of us today. (See Judges 13-16.)

Samson was a promised child, chosen before the foundation of the world, ordained and appointed to deliver the children of Israel from the oppression, obsession, suppression, and captivity of the Philistines. He underestimated the power of prayer on good days, but acknowledged the same power of prayer on his dark days. He traded his connection to God for connection with a woman and was more sensitive to the voices of the children of men than the voice of God; thus, he labored *for* God, but not *with* God. He chose to operate in the flesh, allowing his fleshly lust and desires, and the craving of his soulish passion to lead and direct his path instead of God.

Samson's Connectivity to Men

Samson loved and developed a strong intimacy with Delilah, which polluted and corrupted his love and intimacy with God, just like your phone connection can pollute and corrupt your prayer connection today. Samson's relationship with the children of men, especially with Delilah, was more precious in his sight than his relationship with the God who called and commissioned him to be a deliverer. The glory Samson sought and longed for was the glory of the flesh, which faded away in the twinkling of an eye when his hair was shaved by the hands of his enemies. The devil knew the exact thing to mess with in the life of Samson to bring him and his ministry under his evil dominion. I tell you the truth: The devil knows your weaknesses, and he knows that if he can disconnect your prayer line, he can mess with your life for as long as he is in possession of the remote control for your life's scenes and events.

He traded the anointing of God upon his life for the love of a woman, Delilah. Delilah was called, ordained, anointed, appointed, and commissioned by Satan to steal Samson's power and destroy his relationship with God, and kill his ministry, to the point of his physical death. When the ministry of Samson started, it began with a great passion and God's power. The Philistines dreaded him. Samson was soon distracted by his connectivity to men and was obsessed with the lust of the flesh and lust of his eyes, and his ministry became corrupted and driven by human senses.

While Samson was traveling on the wide and beautiful road, life was sweet and full of fun. His pleasures and splendor made him believe that he had it all under control, forgetting that he was sent to conquer the enemy, not to become immorally involved. Samson broke the edge (his spiritual walls were broken), and he was beaten by the serpent (Satan's agent in human clothing). Samson was conquered by the enemy God sent him to conquer. Though he possessed great powers, physical strength, and the anointing of God, he did not exercise self-restraint. Samson's love for Delilah was crazy, out-of-control love, and he soon forgot about the need for total reliance on God and the leading of His Spirit. Samson began to operate his life and ministry independent of God's rules and standards. Samson became vulnerable and fell prey. He chose to please the children of men—Delilah, in particular— and he followed the pages of his lust instead of God's ordinance. How about you—have you become prey to the enemy God has placed under your feet? Are you a slave to money, talent, or whatever it is that you passionately love?

Are We Better Than Samson?

Samson was a man of like passion, a child of God like you and me. Are we better than Samson? No, not at all. I believe he possibly would have accomplished more for God if He was more firmly connected to God than he was with the children of men. He was ordained to wipe out the Philistines from existence, but he made room for distractions that wiped out his ministry and life. The glory, power, and anointing of the Lord departed from Samson not because God was through with him, but because he lost his first love, his passion, intimacy, and zeal for the Lord, to the lust of the eye, the lust of the flesh, the pride of life, and the glory of this world.

What if Samson was a prayerful man? I believe his many prayers would have delivered him from the many temptations Satan threw at him. Samson's failure to pray resulted in his fall. There was no prayer stored up in Graceland to help him at the hour of temptation. (Failing to pray is just like failing to plan, which will result in planning to fail.) Just reading the book of Judges, from chapter 13 through 16, I noticed that there was never a time when Samson prayed when he was in trouble that God did not answer Him. Samson's life and ministry were cut short because he failed to abide in the secret place of the Most High God, so it was difficult for him to dwell under the shadow of the Almighty.

How about you—how is your prayer life? How is your relationship with God? Have you lost your passion, hunger, intimacy, zeal, and love for the Lord? You are not better than Samson. He was human, and he was not perfect—just like you and me. Samson became a prey because he lost his connection with God to his human connection. How is your phone connection versus your prayer connection? Is your connection to men via your phone more precious than your connection to God in prayer? You do not want to be like Samson, whose prayerlessness robbed him of his powerful legacy, life, and ministry. You must guard your prayer life jealously because you cannot grow above your prayer life.

The Devil

The devil is not worried about your connectivity to men. He is fearful and worried when you are becoming very well connected to God because if you become anointed, his evil kingdom will be in serious trouble. The devil knows if you ever get anointed, his evil mission in your life, family, and ministry will be less effective. The closer you get to God or to being effectively prayerful, the more hindrances and limitations Satan throws at you. Satan's kingdom will not be affected by the many hours you talk on the phone, surf the Internet, or play games. Satan's kingdom will, however, be affected when you become prayerful and do the will of God.

Before Samson became a backslider, he was an effective vessel in the hand of God. Everything changed when he met Delilah. Maybe he thought he could enjoy himself for a while and then make it up with God later, until he got caught up in the journey of no return, which is the game of death. God had great plans for Samson's life—and so did the devil. God provided everything Samson needed to live a fulfilled life and accomplish all his God-given purposes, and the devil provided false hope and distractions in hopes of destroying Samson's testimony by preventing him from finishing well and strong.

Prayer life experience: Satan would do everything he could to use what you love the most to attract you and take you out of God's presence or withstand your hunger to pray. All the devil wants is your undistracted attention to the cares of life. Samson gave Delilah his uninterrupted attention, which he did not give to God. God needs your uninterrupted attention during worship, prayer, and fellowship with Him. Some of us pay serious attention to hearing the voices of men, just as Samson took great delight in hearing the voice of Delilah. As for the voice of God, we are too much in a hurry to go about our business. Our passion for earthly success, fame, and the pressure put on us by the many bills we have to pay obsess our soul. All of the above constitute a stumbling block that could hinder us from hearing the voice of God. When it is time to pray, we are too weak to pray but never too weak to converse or relate to the children of men via our phones.

Samson Gave in to Pleasure

When we ignore or block our ears from hearing the voice of God, it saddens God's heart, but it gladdens Satan's that he is winning. Jesus Christ is busy praying for you not to fail, whereas Satan, the devil, is doing all he possibly can to make you fail or fall. While Jesus Christ is in heaven praying for you, you are relaxed, having fun, watching the latest movie, and playing instead of praying, like Samson. The devil is determined in his evil heart to bring you down until you are distracted and become his prey. Satan's mission and vision is clearly defined: **"To steal, kill**

and destroy"; he is working diligently to meet his goals.

What is your goal as a child of God? Do you know God's purpose for your life? The devil has not lost his hunger, his passion, and his zeal to steal your eternal destiny from you, or to kill your hunger for God and destroy your success goals, aspirations, and dreams. If he is not able to achieve the above, he will team up with you to waste your time on carnality. It is very possible to be fulfilled in the eyes of the children of men and not be fulfilled in the sight of God. Are you fulfilling God's purpose for your life, or are you wasting away comforting yourself with the many excuses Satan uses to engulf your soul with deception? The devil is very much prepared to daily obsess your soul with unprofitable activities by making you unproductive in the things that will honor the Lord. Will you allow him, or choose to drive him away in prayer?

Samson Came to Himself

It came to pass that Samson became a slave to the people he was called to enslave. He was ridiculed and mocked by his captors until he finally came to himself like the prodigal son. Though blinded physically, emotionally wounded, and spiritually drained, Samson came to terms with himself, his faith, love, and passion for God to restore him. Samson humbled himself before God and cried out unto the God of heaven for mercy and for deliverance out of his misery and torture. Our God, who is rich in mercy, answered him and restored his anointing and strengthened him. God gave him spiritual sight, and the Spirit of God came back to him again for the last time and gave him the strength he needed to get his ultimate victory over the enemies of God and his soul.

Samson's victory at his death was greater than all his previous victories put together because he prayed. Samson's ministry could not continue because he was too wounded to go any further. So he requested of God that he might die with his enemies, and He granted him his request. Samson's journey to celebrity was hijacked by the many distractions he allowed into his life. He became like an actor who was killed by the bad man in a screenplay. The movie of his life ended abruptly. It was, however, unfortunate that Samson did not live to celebrate his last and greatest earthly victory.

Prayer life experience: The best gift you can offer to anybody is prayer. Money is good but cannot save lives. Prayer can save lives. I personally would have been dead and buried long ago if not for the power of prayer and the mercy of God.

Effective Public Praying

Powerful and effective public prayer is not based on how long you pray, the large vocabulary you use, or the eloquence of the prayer. It is based on the power of God's Spirit and the efficacy of the Word of God. A long prayer without a solid faith to back it up is mere good talk. Such long prayers will make people feel good for a while. But a short heartfelt, sincere, faith-conceived, faith-born and processed, passionate, and uncompromising prayer with confidence in God, released from a pure heart, will move heaven into action. Such lively, effectual, genuine, to-the-point prayers, aligned with God's Word, avail much. Satan fears such prayers. He hates those who offer such prayers.

Oh, yes, prayer will make the man that God will use to move the world upward and make Satan bow. Being strong in prayer will make you strong spiritually, unbreakable, and a terror to the kingdom of darkness. The prayer that moves God is not determined by affluent expression or powered through excessive scriptural quotations, nor is it reinforced with shouting, screaming, jumping, or gesticulating. The prayer that moves God is that of faith, poured from a clean heart, void of doubt and unbelief, truly knowing that God is faithful and that He is who He says He is, **"the I Am that I am."**

If you do not have a consistent prayer life in the secret place, you will not have a powerful demonstration of the power of prayer in public. The Bible told how Samson prayed, how the power of God fell upon him, and how his strength was restored. He must have been crying out to God "in the secret place" before that public demonstration occurred.

Chapter 16

You Cannot Grow Above
Your Prayer Life

Prayer helps us to grow spiritually. Our phone connections prosper from our communication and help us develop relationships with people of like passion. Our prayer connection prospers our communication and relationship with God. Our phone connection helps us advance and become relevant to the system of this world. Our phone connection helps us grow strong and become popular to our fellow men, and creates dependency on humankind. Our prayer connection helps us grow stronger in grace, in the knowledge of God, and in spiritual empowerment, and makes God our Source. Your prayer connection to God places you above principalities and the powers of wickedness in the air. Your prayer connection will help you abide in the secret place of the Most High, which also will keep you under the shadow of the Almighty.

As you grow in spiritual status, you will be empowered by the Spirit of God. When you become anointed, you will become untouchable; you and your children will be made for signs and for wonders. God's anointing will cost you everything, but will give you everything you will ever need to abide with God. If you have God, you have everything, but what will it profit you if you gain the whole world and lose your soul to the glory of this world? Three things God requires from you and me are:

1. To worship Him in Spirit and in truth.
2. To be totally obedient to His Word and to be prayerful.
3. To serve humanity well and by making disciples for His kingdom, to reach the world for Him.

Prayer life experience: Little praying will produce little results, and prayer without ceasing produces results without limits. First Thessalonians 5:17 says, **"Pray without ceasing."** Fervent prayers prevent programmed problems packed purposefully by the devil against any faithful and committed child of God. Jesus said, "Pray so you do not fall into temptation." Satan says, "Do not pray. Sleep on, and fall into temptation." Prayer will not stop you from been tempted, but prayers can certainly help you overcome the temptations that Satan throws at you. God has promised to answer prayers, if you pray. God has promised to bless you, if you will obey Him. God has promised to help you, if you would trust Him and rely on His faithfulness, not on your own understanding and power. The devil has vowed to stop you from praying, obeying, and trusting God's faithfulness with passion. If Satan can suppress the fire of your prayer, he can oppress your soul. You must make up your mind to pray like Daniel did, even though your life is at risk, or like Esther, who had to go before the king against all odds, putting her life on the line for her people, God's people.

My friend, this one thing I know for sure: If you sincerely and faithfully pray, you can win. God has never lost any fight, and He will never lose any battle. You will not lose any fight if you are passionately and intimately connected to God. He will fight for you. The battle belongs to Him in the first place (if you are a faithful child), and you shall hold your peace. If you stay rooted in His Word and firmly connected to Him, He will build you up, and the gates of hell will not prevail against you.

Much Prayer, Much Grace

Many are the afflictions that the righteous have to go through, but the Lord delivers the righteous from them all. Many are the plans of the devil against the children of God, but the many prayers of the saints in the name of Jesus by the power of the Holy Spirit will deliver these children from all the devil's plans. Much prayer produces much grace; less prayer produces less grace. The grace of God abounds toward us when we are connected to God alone—not the children of men—as our Source. The power of prayer is unlimited. The fruits that prayer produces are timeless, though it all depends on our obedience to God and His instituted authorities, and the level of our faith.

Productive prayer is bonded to the operations of your faith, believing that God is who He says He is, faithful and true. Satan is ready to offer you all the world's pleasures, entertainment, and fantasies at the expense of your eternal life and prayer connection. Whether or not you pray, Satan will trouble you, so why not pray? Maybe your prayers can keep him far away from messing with your life, family, and circle of influence. Satan lives with us in this world; he was cast down to earth. He has no other place to go until he is judged and sentenced, and imprisoned on the Lord's Day. The battles we fight with the devil and his evil hosts are lifelong ones, until we meet Jesus Christ face to face. "So He said to them, **'This kind can come out by nothing but prayer and fasting'** " (Mark 9:29, emphasis added).

Prayer life experience: As relationships are born every day, relationships also are destroyed every day. Sweet talk, good looks, big names, gift buying, and money can only add colors to any relationship. It is the power of prayer from a sincere heart, the oil of thanksgiving from a grateful heart that appreciates God's goodness, from a humble heart, void of selfish interests and manipulation, that can preserve any relationship for a lifetime, till death do you part. The family and friends that pray together will stay together by God's grace.

Prayer is the greatest armor and the greatest privilege we enjoy as children of God. It is the machinery that holds everything in place. Prayer is our means of transport to greater heights, to everything that God is. Prayer transports us to everything God has for us, everything God wants us to be, and everything God wants to do with us in Him, with Him, and through us for Him. Prayer is the driver of our spiritual vehicle, love is the engine, and obedience to God is the accelerator, or gas. It is good to relate to men, but it is far better to relate to God, who causes the children of men to bless us and assist us as needed. We can only love one another with our imperfect minds and hearts. God's love for us is pure and divine, void of selfish interests. We cannot abide in men's bosom for too long without them becoming weary, worried, and worn out. We can only abide in Christ and Christ alone. He is the vine, and we are His branches, for in Him we live, move, and have our being.

Pray About Everything

Learn to pray about everything, even for little things that you think are less important. Believe it or not, those little things are connectors; they complete our joy. Pray for unfriendly friends, that they might know God and embrace the love of God. Who knows if the person you despise today will become your miracle link tomorrow? Never deal with anyone in an attempt to take undue advantage of him or her. Those who do such things are immature and lack the fear of God. Partiality and selfishness hinder prayers. If you must be a hero in the kingdom of God, you must be a God lover, a faithful servant, and one who works by faith, not by sight, for faith operates through the power of love.

Be prayerful, and work out your salvation with fear (reverence). Be obedient to God, who called you to glory and virtue. Prayer is a lifetime treasure that money cannot afford. Be courageous when you pray, and the God who answers by fire will help you. The glory of prayer will sometimes manifest itself at your turning point. Just when it seems all hope is lost, you will see the fourth man in your burning fiery furnace if you persevere. We serve a faithful God. Wait on Him. Though He tarries, He will not be late. God is always on time. We miss it because we want things done according to our timing, not His. Do not give up your confidence; God will make all things beautiful for you in His timing and cause all things to work together for your benefit. Prayer is our shield, our defense, against the wiles of the devil and the wickedness of the hearts of men. There is nothing too big or too small to pray about. We must learn to pray for everything every time, as much as we possibly can pray, by the grace of God.

Prayer life experience: "Don't worry about anything; instead, pray about everything. Tell God what you need, and thank him for all he has done. If you do this, you will experience God's peace, which is far more wonderful than the human mind can understand. His peace will guard your hearts and minds as you live in Christ Jesus" (Philippians 4:6-7 NLT).

Chapter 17

Be Connected to God

The only power that moves God is the power of prayer. If your prayer cannot move God, God will not move men or anything. When you are connected to God, He connects you to your destiny. If the devil can stop you from praying, he can stop you from living fully for God. If the devil succeeds in hindering you from praying daily, he also could hinder you from enjoying the blessings of God. Prayer changes things for good, and all things are possible to him or her who believes in the power of prayer. Do not underestimate the power of God.

Some of Satan's greatest weapons are doubt, selfishness, lust, pride, and deception. If anyone is a doubter, let him or her not think that he or she will receive anything from God because the person who doubts is like the waves of the sea, driven and tossed around by the winds of unbelief. A double-minded person is unstable in all his ways. You must maintain a private line with your God as you do with your phone. Do you think your phone service provider will issue one phone number for two people? I suppose not. The people, who have family packages, all still have their individual phone numbers assigned to them.

Sleeping Warrior

If you are in the habit of asking people to pray for you, now is the time for you to start praying for yourself, too. I am not against people praying for you, nor am I against united prayers; they are wonderful and powerful. But when will you start engaging God for yourself? You cannot be a baby Christian forever. It is time to grow. The apostle Paul said, "When I was a child, . . . I thought [behaved] as a child; but when I became a man, I put away childish things" (1 Corinthians 13:11). It is time for you to rise and shine. Wake up from your slumber. Get up, sleeping warrior. Pray for yourself; do not be at ease in Zion. You will probably pray better for yourself than anyone else can pray for you. You know where you hurt and the struggles you are going through that you probably cannot tell anyone about but God. Have some privacy in prayer, some uninterrupted, undistracted, and relational prayer time with just you and God. Develop a strong intimacy with God. Sometimes go before the Lord just to enjoy His presence. Make no requests; just worship, praise; and adore Him.

When things seem to be difficult, go to God, cry on His shoulder, and cast all your cares upon Him. He loves you and cares about you, and He is willing to perfect all that concerns you. After weeping and pouring out your heart to Him, He will give you peace and show you the way forward. Weeping may last all through the night, but the rivers of joy will flow into your life in the morning if you cast everything on Him. When you team up with God, the enemy will back off. God's hands are always wide open to embrace and accept us in the beloved.

Anytime you are hurting, when the road you are traveling becomes dark, when everyone you know turns his back on you, always remember that it is not over until God says it is. It is the right and the best time for you to turn to God, when men turn their backs on you. He will not leave you helpless, nor will He forsake you. He is a present help in the time of trouble, and He has promised to be with you anytime, any day, anyplace, and any way, both physically and spiritually, as long as you abide in His love and will.

Return to Bethel

Prayer empowers our Christian life and faith. If there was ever a time when prayer was uncompromisingly needed, it is now because the days are evil. We must all begin to train ourselves in the spiritual camp of prayer, as the end draws nearer every day. If we truly seek and honestly long to see sinners saved, discipled, Spirit-filled, and hungry for God, we must return to Bethel to rebuild our prayer altar, which has been destroyed and corrupted with our people-pleasing and pleasure-seeking attitudes. We must again begin to look unto the hills where our help comes from, looking unto Jesus, our prayer Leader, the Author and Finisher of our faith.

Visions are born in prayer; destinies are shaped, spiritual eyes are enlightened, and the revelation of the goodness, the power, and the love of God is revealed. It is also in prayer that the stronghold of the flesh (the yoke of our self-centeredness) will be destroyed. It is in prayer that we will be filled with the fullness of the Holy Spirit, who is the Spirit of prayer Himself.

Break Your Companionship With Your Phone

Your attachment to your phone must be broken. You must never trade your communion, relationship, and fellowship with God for your phone if you are to move forward. You also must tear down the wall of the love of money that has been erected between you and God. Money itself is not bad, but the love of money is the problem. It leads to all kinds of evil. Your phone itself is not bad, but the love of it is a problem. The companionship with it, the dependency on it, and the strong attachment to it are bad. You can talk to the children of men all you want, and it will not make any positive or lasting impact that changes your life or situation significantly. Only God has the power to transform your life, for with Him alone all things (physical or spiritual) are possible.

You must consciously backslide and break free from your companionship with your phone and make God your lifetime companion. If this is not done, it will continue to pose an unavoidable distraction to your sweet communion and connection with God. Jesus Christ gave us instructions on how we should pray undistracted. **"But you [child of God], when you pray, go into your room, and when you have shut your door, pray to your Father who is in the secret place** [key words here are secret, privacy, and uninterrupted]**; and your Father who sees in secret will reward you openly"** (Matthew 6:6).

Faith

Jesus asked, "When the Son of man returns, will He find faith on the earth?" When He comes back, will Jesus find you faithful, doing what He called you and commissioned you to do? I pray He will not find you flying with the wings of the morning, pursuing the cares of this world with an unquenchable passion. Jesus Christ was truly concerned about you and me. We should not take His sacrifice of love, pain, and death on the cross for granted. As Christians without prayer, we will become more and more vulnerable to the attack of the devil daily in our individual lives and families. Some of us put our trust more in the armor of God than in the God who gave us the armor. In ancient times, the ark of the covenant of God meant nothing without the presence of God in it. If your prayer lacks faith, it can do nothing, for faith is the substance of things hoped for, the evidence of things not seen.

Prayer life experience: Do not waste your time praying until you have enough faith to believe in the God who answers prayers.

Prayerlessness

As the engine never moves until you start the car, sinners will not be moved to God until we pray. All the church's good preaching and fun-centered worship, and the cold calls we make to follow up on new converts, will not move the church upward to God. Our phone connections to the children of men are mere human relationship building and development that attract little or no spiritual benefits. Any relationship without the movement of the Spirit of God at the center of it will not move the preacher or his congregation toward God. Prayerlessness kills, and its symptoms are worse than those of HIV. HIV destroys its victims one at a time, but prayerlessness makes room for the devil to come into our homes, our businesses, our cities, and our nations. It is like handing Satan the keys to steal, kill, and destroy at will.

A prayerless church is a powerless church, and a prayerless Christian is a powerless Christian. If we fail to pray, we plan to fail God, fail humanity, and fail ourselves. In this end time, as in the Acts of the apostles and at other times when the people of God honestly and selflessly embraced the love of God with brokenness and in fervency of prayer brought down the power of God to invade the earth, we must feed our passion with prayer, our prayer with faith, and our faith with the power of God's Word.

Do Not Be Too Lazy to Pray

Laziness is not and will never be an excuse for prayerlessness. Do not wait until Satan visits your business, your job, your health, and your family before you can be strong in prayer. Prevention is better than a cure. Must you wait till after the damage is done to take your stand in prayer? God forbid. Please be prayerful. Satan is watching you closely; do not let Satan take undue advantage of your prayerlessness and laziness to advance his evil passion. Do not take prayer life for granted because you are too lazy to pray. **"Men ought always to pray, and not to faint"** (Luke 18:1b, KJV).

Oftentimes our dependence on the children of men and human inventions reduces our dependence on God. It is purely impossible to connect other men to God if you are not well connected to God yourself. You cannot serve God and mammon, nor can you be connected to God in prayer and to your phone at the same time. Make your phone your servant, and make prayer your ministry. As children of God, you and I have no other weapons for warfare but the Word of God, prayer, and praise. Anything that can keep you away from praying or praising God is capable of keeping you away from the very essences of life. Prayer is the life wire that connects you and me to God; God's Word is the connector. You may become prey to the very devil you have been praying against if you do not break your companionship with your phone and firmly connect to God in prayer and in holiness.

Put Your Trust in God

Prayer is the hand that operates our weapons of war against the powers of darkness, and the armor of God is the ammunition with which we fight and clothe ourselves. Some trust in chariots (strong human connection), and some in horses (money, human inventions), but we will remember the name of the Lord our God. Yes, the Lord is our Shepherd; we shall not want. Even though we walk through the valley of the shadow of death, we will fear no evil, for God is with us; His rod and His staff will comfort us. The Lord will prepare a table before us in the presence of our enemies. He will anoint our heads with oil till our cups begin to overflow. We will not trust in the arm of the flesh or in our connection to the children of men, but in the Lord our God. The Lord will not withhold His tender mercies from you, nor will He withhold any good thing from you. The Lord will answer your prayers and satisfy you with His goodness. The Lord will perfect all that concerns you, if you can pray, if you can only truly trust and obey Him.

Chapter 18

God Cannot Fail

God cannot fail, and prayer will not fail, as long as you pray without doubt and in accordance with the Word of God. Let not your heart be troubled. Believe in God. Believe also in the power of prayer. God is faithful; He will not let you down. God will make all things work together for your good. Stop weeping or crying like those who do not have hope. Instead, pray. Our God is a mighty warrior. He is great in battle. He has not failed before, and I know for sure He will not start failing because of you. Be strong. Be of good courage. The God of Israel is still alive, and He will fight if you doubt not. He will pluck your feet off the misery clay and plant your feet on the rock to stay. Cast all your cares upon Him and trust Him to work it all out for you. Put on your garment of praise, and keep praising God.

Fear not, and do not be discouraged. Thinking about your problems will never solve them, but praying about them will move heaven to move your mountains. If God cannot do it, He will not promise it. Do not make room for fear or become negative in your confession; rather, let your confession agree with all the prayers you have prayed. Give no place to the devil through your negative confession, so the accuser, the devil, will not find fault and reasons to delay the produce of your prayer. The devil cannot stop God from doing anything He wants to do, but you can by your negative confession. If your confession is negative, it gives the devil the right and the power to prosper in his evil deeds. As heaven honors your word, so does hell. While the earth remains and until the end of all things, the power of prayer will continue to be our lifeline to God.

Prayer life experience: Any sacrifice made by anyone to pray is never a waste. It is the sacrifice of love and life. Your phone had a price tag on it when you bought it. Prayer is priceless and powerful, and able to preserve you, your household, and all that concerns you.

Jesus' Earthly Ministry

It is the power of prayer that connects our lives to God's will. Prayer helps us overcome our human desires. It is the power of prayer—not our many ritualistic, fun activities—that will bring down the glory of God to our churches. The world can resist our human abilities, but cannot resist the glory of God. If we are to win unbelievers, backsliders, and the undecided in our churches to God through the name of Jesus Christ, by the power of the Holy Spirit, we must do what Jesus did; He lived a life of prayer regularly with His Father. Are you called of God? Are you a true servant of God? What are you doing, and where are you? God is seeking a man, a woman, a boy, a girl to stand in the gap, to pray for His people, to intercede for the unsaved and for the many backsliders in our churches.

Are you available for the Lord to use for His purpose and saving mission on earth? God saved you to serve. He called you, chose you, cleansed you, sanctified you, and anointed you. He ordained and appointed you to go tell it on the mountains and in the valleys that Jesus Christ is Lord. God is calling you to pray, to stand in the gap, for your home, family, town, state, and nation. God did not call you to stay on the phone, surf the Internet, or play games when the devil is leading souls to hell every minute. Are you just going to sit around and let the souls Jesus died for perish? The mission field is not in faraway land; your mission field is your neighbors and your coworkers.

When you are faithful in little, God will commit more into your hands. Stop traveling abroad for missions while souls are languishing in your neighborhood. I am not saying foreign mission is bad, but fortify your home first, then go farther to accomplish more for the Lord. If you abandon your home mission, you have abandoned your call of duty. All I am saying is, Get up and start something. Go evangelize your neighborhood. In God's army, there is no place for those who just want to sit around doing nothing. No. Get up, sleeping soldier. You have your mouth; use it to pray. Let everything that has breath praise the Lord, says the Scripture, and I say unto you by the Spirit of God, Let every man and woman that has breath embrace the power of prayer. The more powerful you are in prayer, the more powerful you will become spiritually. If you are prayerless, you will be powerless and unfruitful, but if you are prayerful, you will be powerful and fruitful in both physical and spiritual matters.

> So I sought for a man among them [the body of Christ] who would make a wall [who will oppose or limit Satan], and stand in the gap before Me on behalf of the land, that I should not destroy it; but I found no one [or anyone who is willing to step out by

faith, totally trust in Me, and uncompromisingly is ready to take his or her stand in prayer, fasting, and making intercession for the people.]
Ezekiel 22:30

How Well Are You Connected?

Is there anything that you will allow to separate you from the love of God? Have you fallen to the level of loving to talk more to men than to your God? How well are you connected to God in prayer, fasting, Bible study, worship, and evangelism? How does that connection compare to your phone connection, your communication with the children of men, and your devotion to television, games, and the Internet? All the world has to offer you is the pride of life, the lust of the flesh, and the lust of the eyes. God is calling; He is calling you into a prayer business to deliver the souls of the children of men from the hands of the power of darkness.

Prayer life experience: Learn to mix your faith with God's Word whenever you come before the Lord in prayer. Always offer your prayer in humility to God. Begin by giving thanks, and end by giving thanks. If you do, soon you will be giving thanks. If Jesus did all He could to lead a life of prayer, why not you, my friend? PRAY. Though Jesus is God and God's only begotten Son, He was always humble and thankful to God. He never took prayer for granted, not once. Are you taking your prayer life for granted?

We Are at War

The devil does not fear people who can just talk; the devil fears those who are addicted to prayer, obedient to God, and on fire for God. Believe it or not, we are at war. The devil is out to sabotage relationships, marriages, and the families of those who choose to live wholly for God, according to His divine purpose and will. The devil is roaming about like a roaring lion seeking whom to devour. The devil is a vicious predator, and those without God's covering are the devil's prey. Satan is working very hard to bring all those under God's covering, or protection, into temptation so they can sin and fall from grace, that he might be able to bring them under his subjection.

God has given you power over Satan and sin if you can pray, rely on His faithfulness, be led by His Spirit, and not doubt. You and I can bring Satan to judgment in so many areas of our lives by the power of the Word of God and the power of our prayer when our obedience is complete. Your prayer will be unstoppable if you can develop a stronghold of prayer. God is calling on you to give prayer its proper place in your life. God is saying, "Stop trading your prayer connection for your phone connection." God wants you to break your companionship, your intimacy, with your phone and develop a passionate love and intimacy with Him and for Him alone. You are God's glory in Christ Jesus and you are under a divine mandate to lead and live your life to the glory of God if God is truly your Father and Lord as you claim. If your phone line is very, very active, how about your prayer line, is it very active? If you cannot do without your phone on a daily basis, why are you living your daily live without praying?

Chapter 19

We Need Revival

The revival we are longing for will not come until we get the victory in the spirit, and it begins by humbling ourselves before God on our knees. Nevertheless, my friend, the foundation of God stands sure. Oh, yes, the Lord knows those that are His. If you decide to surrender completely to God, your faith, love, and fear of God will be tested, refined by the fire of adversity, purified, and sanctified by the blood of the Lamb of God. You must pass the test before God can trust you with His power and anointing. The devil will test you to see how much you really love God and fear Him, and if you are willing to give God your "Isaac." The "Isaac" in your life is that thing you love most. It could be your phone, your job, your earthly goods, or wealth. Abraham obeyed God and was willing to give God his Isaac; thus, he was called God's friend because of his faith and unquestionable obedience. Will you obey God and lay down your Isaac at His feet? Your faith, love, and fear of God will be proved. The question is not whether the test will come, but when tested, whether you will pass the test.

Prayer life experience: If you do not pray, you become prey, vulnerable to all kinds of satanic attacks, influences, and deception. God forbid, you will allow

Satan to make your life and home a testing ground because of your prayerlessness, in Jesus' name.

Pray—You Have No Excuse!

I urge you in the name of God, if you have a phone line, please make sure you have a prayer line. If you do not have a phone line, you still need to have a prayer line, for your destiny, your breakthroughs, and your progress in life may depend on the power of your prayers. Your faith, trust, and positive confession are vital as far as your prayer life, or line, is concerned. If you really want to build a stronghold of prayer in your life, you must begin now—today, not tomorrow. Your prayer line is your miracle link, able to take you above and beyond the odds of life. God is faithful to His Word. Learn to confess God's Word over your life. Your positive confession must be in total agreement with your prayer for a breakthrough to bring in your prayer harvest. Let your prayer life be hot and spicy, too hot for the devil and his evil hosts to handle.

Prayer life experience: Never plan before you pray; always pray for guidance and direction before you plan. God will not give birth to what He did not conceive, nor will He be strong for you if you do not make room for Him. Jesus prayed for Peter not to fall, but Peter did not pray for himself. Peter fell into temptation because it takes two to agree in prayer for prayer to prevail. If not for God's abundant mercy and love, Peter would have gone fishing for fish the rest of his life instead of fishing for souls. Jesus had to return to Peter to restore and reconnect him and the rest of the apostles back to Jesus through communion fellowship, even the breaking of bread. Pray for yourself. The power of your prayers is priceless.

Put God First

As children of God, we must put God first in our lives before all our plans, pursuits, and dreams. A very good and faithful child of God is called to be a good soldier, and will have no other option but to be faithful to God. If you are one of the faithful ones, you have no choice but to obey God. A good and faithful follower will not give room for or allow anything to interfere with his or her master's duty, business, or services. A good follower seeks to accomplish his or her master's mission, perfectly and timely. A good soldier wants to please his superior and will do whatever he or she is asked to do decently and in order. He must be the first and the last in your life, as a child of the Most High God. Make Him your "Alpha and Omega." Develop your intimacy with God in prayer, for the weapons of your warfare are not carnal, but mighty through God to the pulling down of strongholds. Your exclusive communication with the children of men, counting on men, staying on the phone and on the Internet, or playing games will not pull down any demonic stronghold, but make them even stronger. Prayer changes things, for all things are possible for those who believe.

Prayer life experience: Be warned and beware, my brethren, of the many devices of the devil. The devil will do all he possibly can to occupy your daily life with the consuming zeal for materialism. Jesus Christ indeed said, "Occupy till I come." He was not talking about the glory of this world; He was talking about taking your rightful place in God, in the circle of life, and in prayer. If you want to grow and fully occupy till Jesus comes back, you must live a life of prayer.

General Phone Caution

1. If you have been gossiping via your phone, stop doing it.

2. Do not vent your anger through the phone or in anger tell anyone words that are hard to bear via your phone. The person you are talking to might be driving and become a road hazard. Some people lose control when they get angry.

3. Reduce your phone usage while you are driving, especially when you are not in a good mood, when you are sick, when it is raining, or anytime the weather is bad.

4. Put your phone on vibration, especially when you are in church, prayer meetings, or any gatherings. Stop distracting or disturbing people with your "Hello, can you hear me now?" It will not cost you anything to be nice and polite, get up, leave the area, and then talk all you want privately. If you cannot abuse your phone usage at your workplace or while you are before your boss, why must you do it in the house of God? God never said, "My house shall be called **a house of answering phones.**" God only said, "My house shall be called **the house of prayer**" for all people.

5. Start giving the attention you give to your phone to the Spirit of God, your spiritual growth, your prayer life, and Bible study. God loves you. He always wants to talk with you every time you come before Him in prayer. Stop your hurried attitude whenever you are in His presence. Let God enjoy your presence and your undivided attention in His presence. Learn to enjoy God's voice as you have learnt to enjoy the voice of the children of men.

6. When you are praying and your phone rings, let it ring. If the call is important, the person will call again. Stop doing to God what you cannot do to your human leaders; don't hang up your prayer line on Him. If it is an emergency, be polite and respectable in God's

presence. Ask to be excused for a minute as you attend to your fellow men if you must take the call. Stop taking God for granted. Stop disrespecting Him every time your phone rings when you are in His presence.

7. Develop a good phone manner as well as a good prayer manner. Make your prayer line—not your phone line—a priority line. Be connected to God, but relate with men. If you are not yet on God's prayer network, please get connected today, and let God begin the process of connecting you to your destiny.

8. Please do not drive and talk on the phone in any school zone or children's park. Form the habit of being safety-conscious anytime you are driving in a school zone or an area where children are playing. Please be alert. Put away your headset, handset, or Bluetooth when driving during busy intersections and areas with pedestrians, Refrain from using your phone as much as possible.

Prayer life experience: When you are praying, do not be selfish with your prayers; pray for others the same way you would passionately pray for yourself. The second greatest commandment is to love your neighbor as you love yourself, which includes praying for others as you pray for yourself.

Final Note

If you have a phone line, do you have a prayer line? If you enjoy talking to men, do you enjoy talking to God? Your phone line will move you toward the children of men and transforms you into the likeness of men. But your prayer line will move you toward God and transforms you into the likeness of God. Your phone line improves and enhances your relationship with and dependency on the children of man, but your prayer line improves and enhances your relationship, communion, and dependency on God. Your phone line will help you connect and stay connected to men who want to be connected to you, but your prayer line will help you connect and stay connected to God, who is willing to connect to all men. Your connection to men ends when they die, for if all your hope and trust is in men, you are of all men most miserable. Your phone number is not yours; you are just renting or leasing it. But your prayer life is free; it is your lifeline to God.

Forever Connected

Your connection to God will never end if you are faithfully and firmly connected. Since God will never die, when you die, you have hope; your connection to God is not lost. The choice is yours, my friend. There is a way that seems right, but it ends in destruction. Joshua said, "As for me and my household, we will serve the Lord." Joshua was determined to stay connected to God and to God alone forever. Your phone is helpful to you, no doubt, but do not ever let your phone get in the way of your communion, relationship, and fellowship with God for any reason. God said, "My glory I will not share with any other god, anything, or anyone." God will not and cannot share you, "His glory," with your phone, the Internet, or games. There is a time for everything under the sun. There is a time to pray, and there is a time to talk on the phone, browse the Internet, and play games. Never trade your prayer time for any of the above, and do not let the devil manipulate your life so you begin to play when you ought to be praying. Never underestimate the power of prayer. Prayer gave Jesus the victory and will do the same for you. We are at war. The devil longs to destroy us with a passion. He is working very hard to achieve his evil goal in our lives. Will you let the devil have his way in your life, or will you put on the garment of prayer and pray? Beware, and be careful—the devil is watching. He is very smart; he will make good use of any loopholes (opportunities) you give him in your life, family, and ministry.

The Toll-free Number to Call Is J-E-S-U-S!

Connect your prayer line to Jesus Christ today! If you need ANYTHING OR HAVE ANY QUESTIONS ABOUT WHAT IS GOING ON IN YOUR LIFE, please feel free to call heaven's toll free number: J-E-S-U-S. God is ready twenty-four seven to answer your call. God will never turn any caller away, nor will His spiritual prayer line network be busy so you cannot connect. The good thing about God's prayer line network is that you can call God from anywhere, anytime, as long as you believe and have the faith to call. You are just a minute away from your next level in life if you will call heaven today.

Go Ahead and Call Now

God will bless you if you call Him today. You have nothing to lose, but you have everything to gain. The call is free, so why not now? You do not have to wait till tomorrow or next week to call. Call right now. He is standing by to answer your call. If you call now, you will be forever glad you did. Please get on your knees and call J-E-S-U-S now!

May God bless your connection and answer all your doubtless, faith-born, and faith-processed prayers, in Jesus' mighty name. The toll-free number to call again is J-E-S-U-S. Call now. Remember, your prayer line is your miracle link. Prayer is our lifetime duty on earth. You will never retire from prayer, and as long as the earth remains, you and I must pray without ceasing. I love you. I pray that God blesses you, keeps you from evil, and perfects all that concerns you and your family, in Jesus' name. Amen!

Contact the Author

Contact this author for speaking engagements or book signings. Call or e-mail Pastor Joseph Blessing Omosigho anytime at the information below. He is a God-sent speaker, preacher, teacher, mentor, author, and songwriter.

The Ministry of Christ
P.O. Box 292924
Lewisville, TX 75029-2924
214-994-8080
E-mail: ministryofchrist@gmail.com
Website: endtimemission.org

May God perfect all that concerns you, give you peace, and surround your life with His favor, and bless your prayer life [line] in Jesus' name. Please, call or write, share your prayers and testimonies with us, we love to hear from you and rejoice with you. Also, please, send your donations and love gift to the address above or online at our website, to help us reach the world for Jesus Christ. Please, do not send us any donations or gifts if you are not lead by the Lord. God loves you and we do too. Peace be unto you and your household in Jesus name.